Mozart: his life and times

MOZART

his life and times

Peggy Woodford

Paganiniana Publications, Inc.
211 West Sylvania Avenue, Neptune City, N.J. 07753

To Imogen

ISBN 0-87666-643-8

Published by PAGANINIANA PUBLICATIONS, INC.
211 West Sylvania Avenue
Neptune City, New Jersey 07753

Contents

Acknowledgements

The Editor and Publishers would like to thank the following for kindly granting permission to quote extracts:

Macmillan (Emily Anderson, *The Letters of Mozart*)
Secker & Warburg (Erich Schenk, *Mozart and His Times*)

The illustrations have mostly come from original prints and engravings or from private collections. Grateful thanks, however, are due to the following for kindly granting reproduction rights:

Beethoven-Haus, Bonn
Bibliothèque du Conservatoire, Paris
British Museum, London
City Music Library, Leipzig
Gesellschaft der Musikfreunde, Vienna
Grenoble Museum
Karl Marx University, Leipzig
Library of Congress, Washington
Liceo Musicale, Bologna
Musée Condé, Chantilly
Oxford University Press
Royal College of Music, London
Salzburg Mozarteum
Salzburg Museum
Universitätsbibliothek, Tübingen
University of Edinburgh
University of Glasgow

Wadhurst, January 1977   A.O.

Bibliography

Anderson, Emily, *Letters of Mozart and his Family*, 2 vols., rev. (London 1966)

Auden, W. H., Chester Kallman, *et al., Great Operas of Mozart* (New York 1962)

Blom, Eric, *Mozart* (London 1935)

— *Mozart's Letters* (Harmondsworth 1956)

Blume, Friedrich, *Classical and Romantic Music* (New York 1970, London 1972)

Brion, Marcel, *Daily life in the Vienna of Mozart and Schubert* (London 1959)

Burk, J. N., *Mozart and his music* (New York 1959)

Dent, E. J., *Mozart's Operas* (London 1913, rev. ed. 1947)

Einstein, Alfred, *Mozart* (London 1946)

Gal, Hans, *The Golden Age of Vienna* (London 1948)

Girdlestone, C. M., *Mozart's Piano Concertos* (London 1948)

Hollis, Helen Rice, *The Piano* (Newton Abbot 1975)

Hughes, Spike, *Famous Mozart operas* (London 1957)

Hutchings, Arthur, *A Companion to Mozart's Piano Concertos* (London 1948)

Kenyon, Max, *Mozart in Salzburg* (London 1952)

— *A Mozart letter book* (London 1956)

King, A. Hyatt, *Mozart in Retrospect* (London 1955)

Landon, H. C. R., Mitchell, D., *et al., The Mozart Companion* (London 1956)

Landon, H. C. R., *Essays on the Viennese Classical Style* (London 1970)

Pauly, Reinhard G., *Music in the Classical Period* (Englewood Cliffs, New Jersey, 1965)

Schenk, Erich, *Mozart and His Times* (Vienna 1955, New York 1959, London 1960)

Valentin, Erich, *Mozart, a pictorial biography* (London 1959)

Mozart. Portrait in oils by Barbara Kraft, 1819 (Vienna, Gesellschaft der Musikfreunde). This was based on a detail from the family portrait of 1780–81 painted by Croce. According to Otto Erich Deutsch, Kraft worked under Nannerl's supervision: the picture appears to be the best and most faithful likeness of all'

Chapter 1

Growing up in Salzburg

'Mozart is good and admirable'—Beethoven

The house in Salzburg where Wolfgang Amadeus Mozart was born was tall and narrow; it had an elaborately moulded portico over the large front entrance and beautiful

Mozart's birthplace. A drawing. (Schenk, *Mozart and His Times)*

9

The room in which Mozart was born. The Mozart house was acquired by the International Foundation of the Mozarteum in 1917, and is now a notable museum

Salzburg, with the Archbishop's palace, the Cathedral, the Nonnberg Convent and St. Peter's Monastery. A contemporary painting

Prince-Archbishop Sigismund Schrattenbach (1698–1771). A portrait in oils

wrought-iron gate-doors leading into an open hallway. The ground floor was the storeroom of a shop, nothing to do with the Mozarts; their part of the house began at a higher level on the third floor. Today the house faces a street; in the 1750s, however, it looked out over an open square, the Löchelplatz, which, with its sparkling fountain, must have been a pleasant sight. In his biography of Mozart, Eric Blom has left us a fine pensketch of the atmosphere of the place:

The flat-fronted house, with no visible roof, looks Italianate from the outside, but has a Germanic homeliness within. How apt a setting for a master whose manner is Italian, whose soul German. A curious odour strikes the visitor as he enters the whitewashed and roughly paved entrance hall, a smell that makes one think of drains and cats and dinners all in one, without being exactly redolent of any of these things.

The house was stuffed with muscial instruments in every corner; three members of a family of four were full-time musicians. There were violins, harpsichords, clavichords, recorders, and probably sheets of music everywhere. Wolfgang's father, Leopold Mozart (1719–87), was a well-known musician; he played and taught the violin, organ

and clavier; he had written a popular book about playing the violin called *Violin School* (published in the year of Wolfgang's birth) which was widely known and used in the musical world.

Leopold was also the official composer to the Court of Salzburg, a court ruled over at the time of Wolfgang's birth by a Prince-Archbishop called Count Schrattenbach, a good man who encouraged music and the arts, and kept a permanent orchestra of between 21 and 33 musicians. In those days Germany and Austria were divided internally into small city-states, ruled over by electors or princes; each ruler kept up as lavish a court as he could afford, based on the example set by the Emperor in Vienna.

Music was an important part of court life; each court had a *Kapellmeister* who was in charge of all the music, both of the

Leopold Mozart
(1719–87). Frontispiece
to the first edition of
his *Violin School,*
1756

religious music in the chapels and churches, and the music
needed for festivals, balls and receptions. Leopold was
Vice-Kapellmeister, as well as court composer; and the Court
of Salzburg was famous for its music, although it was only a
small court in a small town.

So Leopold was an accomplished musician; and when his son
was born on 27 January 1756, the child lived and breathed in
an atmosphere of music from the start. The little boy was
christened Johan Chrysostom Wolfgang Theophilus; this was
shortened to Wolfgang Amadeus (Amadeus being the Latin
version of the Greek name Theophilus). Leopold called his son
Wolfgangerl or even Woferl, just as he called Wolfgang's elder
sister Nannerl, instead of Anna Maria. Nannerl was five years
older than Wolfgang: she was born in July 1751. There were
other children, but they all died very young: infant mortality
was high in the eighteenth century.

Nannerl was an extremely musical little girl; her father had

Maria Anna ('Nannerl')
Mozart (1751–1829).
The superimposed head
was probably done by
Pietro Antonio
Lorenzoni in 1763.
The rest of the body
and the background
would have been
painted beforehand as
was the custom of the
period. Nannerl married
in 1784. On her
husband's death in
1801 she devoted
herself to teaching in
Salzburg. Becoming
blind in 1820, she died
in poverty

been teaching her the clavier since she was about five, and was delighted with her progress. The 'clavier' was the generic word used in those days in Germany to mean any sort of stringed keyboard instrument, including the clavichord, the harpsichord and the piano.

The clavichord looked like a small piano, rather an odd-shaped one. It had a keyboard like a piano, though it was smaller in range; and it had a very soft tone. A brass blade or tangent struck a string when the clavichord key was pressed, and the harder it was pressed the *higher* in pitch was the note; it was no *louder*. From the early fifteenth century until Mozart's time, the clavichord was held the king of keyboard instruments.

13

German clavichord, 1763

Harpsichord by Johann Adolf Hass of Hamburg, 1764. The instrument was restored in about 1840, which may explain why the natural keys are ivory and the accidentals ebony: normally these colours would have been reversed, with ebony natural keys and ivory accidentals. This instrument appears to have once belonged to Mozart himself. (Russell Collection, University of Edinburgh)

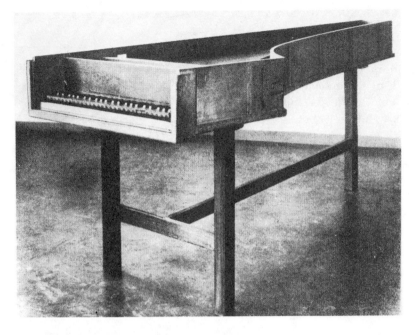

Piano by Cristofori,
Florence 1726
(Leipzig. Museum of
Musical Instruments,
Karl Marx University)

The harpsichord, which has enjoyed such a revival in recent years, is as old as the clavichord, and its strings, which look like those in a piano, are *plucked.* The player, however, has less control over the tone and length of the note he strikes than he does in the clavichord, but the range of notes is larger. There can also be several keyboards or manuals coupled together, as on an organ—a distinctive feature.

The piano, or rather a forerunner of it, was perfected in Florence by an Italian, Bartolomeo Cristofori. In his workshops sometime between 1693 and 1700 he invented an instrument in which the tangents of the clavichord and the plectra of the harpsichord were replaced by a wholly new innovation, a leather-covered hammer which struck the strings. In the process the player could suddenly control and graduate the tone and the duration of a pitch (or note) and, even more dramatically, its *loudness* and *softness.* The early piano was a refined instrument, full of colour and delicate nuances. The Viennese pianos of Mozart's day, unlike their English counterparts further allowed for a light, rapid action with precise damping (or silencing of sound) and correspondingly greater clarity. Early pianos went by various names. Most, however, were known as forte-pianos (later pianofortes), a term that essentially emphasised the ability of the instrument to distinguish between soft (*piano*) and loud (*forte*).

The Mozart household, as we have seen, was from the outset exposed to all kinds of keyboard instruments. When Leopold taught his daughter Nannerl to play the 'clavier' it can

15

Austrian pedal grand piano, probably by Johann Schmidt, late 18th century. Leopold Mozart recommended Schmidt to the Salzburg court and Wolfgang must have been familiar with his instruments (Nürnberg, Rück Collection, Germanisches Nationalmuseum)

accordingly be safely assumed that she probably played most of them, but specifically the harpsichord and forte-piano. She was a hard-working, good-tempered, sweet girl, and Leopold had high hopes for her.

Then, when Wolfgang was four, and a lively, intelligent little boy, he started interrupting Nannerl's lessons. He had already been amusing himself since he was three years old by trying out his own chords and tunes for hours on the clavier, and now he needed to be properly taught. Leopold was amazed by his son's progress; Wolfgang, only four years old, would learn a whole minuet and trio in half an hour. Leopold kept a diary about his family, and there are passages from it which give a vivid picture of what Mozart was really like as a little boy. Evocative recollections are also found in a letter written to Nannerl by one Johann Andreas Schachtner (1732–95), court trumpeter at Salzburg. The letter dates from April 1792, a matter of months after Mozart's death, and is full of anecdotal material:

As soon as he began to give himself to music, all his senses were as good as dead to other activities, and even his pranks and games with toys had to be done to music if he was really going to enjoy them. When he and I carried toys for a game from one room to another, whichever of us was empty-handed had to sing and play a march on the fiddle.

Wolfgang was single-minded about everything he did. When he was learning arithmetic, for instance, he even stopped his music for a while, and in his enthusiasm covered the table, chairs, walls and even the floor with chalked figures. His mother, kind and cheerful, probably cleared it up without much fuss, because Wolfgang was always making her laugh with his unpredictable antics. He was a fiery, affectionate little boy, ready for anything.

From an early stage Wolfgang displayed a remarkable sense of absolute pitch. Schachtner, for instance, tells how he possessed a very good violin,

which Wolfgang always called butter-fiddle on account of its soft and full tone. One day, soon after you returned from Vienna, I let him play on it, and he could not extol it enough. A day or two later I came to see him again, and found him amusing himself with his own violin. At once he said: 'How is your butter-fiddle?' and then went on fiddling away at his improvisation. Finally he reflected a little and

Salzburg. An engraving

17

said to me: 'Herr Schachtner, your violin is tuned half a quarter-tone lower than mine, if you have left it tuned as it was when I last played on it.' I laughed at that, but Papa, who knew the child's extraordinary ear and memory, asked me to fetch my violin and see whether he was right. I did so, and that was how it was.

This same letter of Schachtner's to Nannerl tells us much else besides. For example, Mozart's dislike of wind instruments because of their impure tone:

Almost until his tenth year he had an insurmountable fear of the trumpet when it was played alone, without other music. If one merely held a trumpet toward him, it was like pointing a loaded pistol at his heart. Papa wanted to cure him of this childish fear, and once asked me, in spite of his protests, to blow the trumpet at him. But my God, I wish I had not let myself be persuaded! Almost as soon as Wolfgang heard the blaring tone, he turned pale and began to reel, and if I had continued any longer, he would certainly have fallen into convulsions.

Later in life he came to love the woodwind.

Further in the letter there is an account of Wolfgang's early attempts at composition (he was then four or five):

Once I accompanied your Papa to your house after the Thursday service. We found four-year-old Wolfgangerl busy with the pen.
Papa: 'What are you doing?'
Wolfgang: 'A concerto for the clavier; I'll soon be finished with the first part.'
Papa: 'Let me see; that must be something remarkable indeed!'
Your Papa took it from him and showed me a smear of notes, mostly written over wiped-off ink-blots. . . . We laughed at first over this apparent nonsense, but by and by your father began to notice the main thing, the notes, the composition. For a long time he stood intently studying the sheet of paper, and at last two tears, tears of admiration and delight, fell from his eyes. 'Look at this, Herr Schachtner,' he said, 'how correctly and in good order it is all composed; only it is useless because it is so extraordinarily difficult that no one would be able to play it.' Wolfgangerl put in: 'That's why it is a concerto; you have to practise it until you can do it. See, this is how it ought to go.' He played, but could just bring out enough for us to grasp what he was aiming at. At that time he had the idea that playing a concerto was synonymous with working miracles.

At the same age, Wolfgang also made his first appearance on the stage, as a singer; he sang in an opera, and from that moment onwards opera became one of his passions.

Two years passed, and when Wolfgang was nearly six and Nannerl was eleven, Leopold decided it was time to show his

Munich. An engraving. In the centre is the Frauenkirche and to the right is the Elector's Palace where Wolfgang and Nannerl appeared with such success

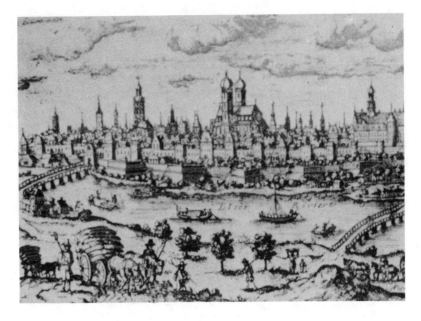

two brilliant children to the world. Both Wolfgang and Nannerl had made such amazing progress that he felt they were wasted in Salzburg. For although Salzburg was in its way a centre of music, and full of clever musicians from France and Italy, as well as Austria and Germany, it was still only a small country town at heart, narrow-minded and unwilling to give genius its full praise.

Leopold decided to take his children on a short tour first; they would spend two weeks or so in Munich, the capital of Bavaria, and if this was successful they would later go farther afield. The Elector of Bavaria held a lavish court at Munich, and there was a large number of musicians attached to it. Every year, in the Carnival season called *Fasching* which lasted from Christmas until Lent, there were endless festivities: operas, concerts, masked balls and parties, fireworks, fairs and all sorts of other amusements.

Leopold decided that this was the best time in which to launch his two children into the gay social whirl of Munich, so in January 1762 the whole family set out.

Before visiting musicians could perform in a city they had to be invited to give a concert by the reigning prince, in this case the Elector of Bavaria, Maximilian Joseph. Fortunately Leopold had the necessary letters of introduction, and a concert was arranged without any trouble. The gay nobility of Munich were agog to hear these two miraculous children play. Wolfgang, just six, was tiny for his age, and Nannerl not very much bigger.

19

The concert consisted of pieces played on the clavier and the violin; of songs by Nannerl; and of a trick performance by Wolfgang, in which the clavier keys were covered with a piece of cloth beneath which he played a piece and then improvised.

The concert was a wild success. People could hardly believe their eyes and ears. The Mozarts became the talking-point of the Carnival, and were invited to all the great houses and palaces to give concerts. Public concerts did not exist in those days—it was not until twenty or so years later that they were introduced in Vienna. Until then musicians relied entirely on the patronage of the nobility.

The success of his two children surpassed Leopold's wildest dreams. Their short period in Munich was one long excitement for Nannerl and Wolfgang. but the highlight for Wolfgang was the Italian opera; for the first time in his life he was taken to hear one. All the fireworks and fun paled into insignificance after that.

Nearly three weeks after their arrival in Munich the Mozart family went back to Salzburg, and Leopold began to plan the future.

Violin used by Mozart in his childhood

Mozart, aged 7

Two views of Vienna by Bernardo Bellotto

Chapter 2

Vienna

'You know that I am, so to speak, swallowed up in music, that I am busy with it all day, speculating, studying, considering'—Mozart to his father

In September 1762, after a few months of preparation in Salzburg, the whole Mozart family set out for Vienna, the capital of Habsburg Austria, one of Europe's most important centres of music, and the city in which the Emperor Francis I and the Empress Maria Theresia held their elaborate court. Vienna had been a city of music since the twelfth century, when Albert I collected together a band of instrumentalists whom he called his Royal Musicians. From then onwards music was an important part of court life; but it was in the seventeenth and eighteenth centuries that music in Vienna had its Golden Age. In the mid-seventeenth century Ferdinand III, a good composer and performer himself, sent his court musicians to study in Italy; Italian opera was first introduced to Vienna, and a great tradition established. For the next hundred years all the Austrian emperors encouraged music in every way; by founding a Musical Academy and by encouraging good teachers; by paying court musicians handsomely, and by encouraging, above all, opera; and by attracting the best singers and performers in Europe to Vienna.

Maria Theresia's father, Charles VI, had one hundred and forty court musicians on his payroll, many of whom accompanied him from city to city when he went on official visits. He loved opera, and had his own daughters' voices trained so that they could sing in operas performed before the court.

In fact, it was with the coming of Maria Theresia to the throne of Austria that music at the Viennese Court began its wane. Perhaps Charles had overdone her musical training until she lost interest in music generally; but whatever the reason,

Maria Theresia (1717–80) with her family. Her consort Francis I is seated on the left and her eldest son, later Joseph II, is standing on her left. Miniature on paper, 1760, after the painting by Martin van Meytens, c. 1752

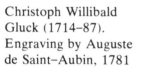

Christoph Willibald Gluck (1714–87). Engraving by Auguste de Saint–Aubin, 1781

few court musicians were employed and less and less Imperial encouragement was given. The nobility took over the role of encouraging and supporting musicians; the famous composer Joseph Haydn spent a peaceful happy life near Vienna as Count Esterházy's *Kapellmeister* for which he received a generous salary. The other most famous composer in Vienna at that time, Gluck, was still on the payroll of the Imperial court as chief composer.

This, then, was the city which lived and breathed music, and which Leopold Mozart hoped his son would conquer. The Viennese Court and nobility, forewarned, were already looking forward to the arrival of this musical prodigy of six years old, Wolfgang Mozart.

The family travelled by river to Vienna, sailing down the Danube on the mail-boat, known as the 'water ordinary'; on each side were beautiful, vine-covered banks. Soon after their arrival in Vienna, Wolfgang and Nannerl gave their first concert in a private palace, and such was its success that a command came immediately from the Emperor and Empress for the children to give a concert next day at the Imperial palace. Someone who was actually at that concert (which in the event was held two days later, on 13 October, the name-day of the Empress Maria Theresia's youngest son) has left a description for us.

Those in the audience could scarcely believe their eyes and ears when the children played. In particular the Emperor Francis I was delighted with the little wizard, as he jokingly called him. He chatted with him many times.

Wolfgang was not at all overawed by all this; and when the Emperor challenged him to play a piece with a single finger, he did not hesitate:

Vienna, 'Am Hof'. On the left is the Collalto Palace where Wolfgang and Nannerl appeared before the Viennese nobility in 1762

Resolutely, he tried it at once, and to everyone's astonishment played several pieces very neatly in this manner. Even at that age he showed a trait in his character which has remained with him ever since; namely, contempt for all praise from high places, and a certain reluctance to play for them if they were not very knowledgeable about music.

23

A scene from the private life of Maria Theresia and her family. Drawing by the Archduchess Marie Christine. The little girl with the doll is Marie Antoinette, the boy in the foreground eating cake is Maximilian who later became Archbishop of Cologne and Beethoven's patron (Vienna Österreiche Nationalbibliothek)

If Wolfgang thought his audience was rather stupid, he would play unimportant easy pieces; but if somebody who really knew and loved music was there, he played with all his heart and soul.

After the concert, the Empress's children showed Wolfgang round the rich state apartments in the palace. One of the princesses was Marie Antoinette, later to be a Queen of France; she took a great fancy to Wolfgang, and when he slipped and fell on a highly polished floor she pulled him to his feet. This pleased Wolfgang because, in general, musicians in those days were treated as part of the servant class, and never had any friendly contact with the nobility. His welcome was exceptional; and he enjoyed himself so much that when he saw the Empress again to say good-bye he 'jumped on her lap, threw his arms round her neck, and kissed her good and thoroughly'. This is his father's description.

For the next week the two children had a crowded programme. On one day, for instance, they gave three concerts. The first was at half past two and went on until four o'clock. A carriage arrived and took them at full gallop to another house, where they stayed until half past five. Then they

The Archduchess Marie
Antoinette (1755–93).
Painting by
Wagenschoen

rushed on to another great house, where the concert did not finish until nine o'clock. Quite exhausted, Wolfgang and Nannerl were taken back to their inn, and the following day the programme was just as energetic.

So under this pressure it was not surprising that at the end of the week, just as they were leaving for another concert at the Imperial palace, Wolfgang suddenly fell ill. In a letter of 30 October 1762 to Johann Lorenz Hagenauer, a Salzburg merchant who was the family's landlord and banker, Leopold wrote:

I was beginning to think that for fourteen days in succession we were far too happy. God has sent us a small cross and we must thank

25

His infinite goodness that things have turned out as they have. At seven o'clock in the evening of the 21st we again went to the Empress. Our Woferl, however, was not quite as well as usual and before we drove there and also as he was going to bed, he complained a good deal of his backside and his hips. When he got into bed, I examined the places where he said he had pain and found a few spots as large as a kreutzer, very red and slightly raised and painful to the touch. But they were only on his shins, on both elbows and a few on his posterior; although there were very few. He was feverish and we gave him a black powder and a margrave powder; but he had a rather restless night. On Friday we repeated the powders both morning and evening and we found that the spots had spread: but, although they were larger, they had not increased in number. We had to send messages to all the nobles, where we had engagements for the next eight days, and refuse for one day after another. We continued to give margrave powders and on Sunday Woferl began to perspire, as we wanted him to, for hitherto his fever had been more or less dry. I met the physician of the Countess von Sinzendorf (who happened to be away from Vienna) and gave him particulars. He at once came back with me and approved of what we had done. He said it was a kind of scarlet fever rash . . . These scarlet fever spots, which are a fashionable complaint for children in Vienna, are dangerous and I hope that Woferl has now become acclimatised.

Wolfgang was in bed for two weeks before he was well enough to get up again. He was small and thin, and had little reserve of strength.

But even in this short period the nobility, always looking for a new sensation, had already lost interest in the child genius. There were fewer and fewer invitations to give concerts in Vienna, and in disgust Leopold decided to take his family back to Salzburg. One very good thing had come out of Vienna, though; an invitation to go on to Paris and Versailles. This cheered them as they travelled in a very cold and draughty carriage back to Salzburg.

In those days everybody who could not afford to run their own carriage and horses used either the post-chaise or mail-coach. The regular mail-coach was the slowest and cheapest form of transport; it went at a snail's pace because the horses were not usually changed each night, so the driver did not dare tire them out. A post-chaise went at twice the speed because fresh horses were used every day, collected at the posting inn where the travellers spent the night. To keep warm, deep straw was put on the floors of the carriages, and besides that, sensible travellers took fur coats and rugs to wrap round their legs. Even so, it was often cold and uncomfortable, especially when rain and wind got in; and a journey which takes us one day by car could take a fortnight then.

Mozart in 1762 at the age of six. He is seen wearing a court suit originally intended for the Archduke Maximilian and given to him by the Empress Maria Theresia. The painting has been attributed to Pietro Antonio Lorenzoni (*cf* his portrait of Nannerl, p. 13)

In fact, the Mozarts found travelling so uncomfortable that Leopold bought a carriage with some of the money earned in Vienna. Wolfgang was delighted: he, being the thinnest, felt the cold most. He also liked the new carriage because it went fast and had good springs.

Back in Salzburg, Wolfgang fell ill again; all his joints were very painful with rheumatism, and he was in bed for a month or so.

An Italian painter called Lorenzoni, who had arrived in Salzburg in the 1740s, wanted to paint Wolfgang and Nannerl. They both wore the court clothes the Emperor had given them in Vienna; Wolfgang's was of fine lilac-coloured silk, trimmed with wide double braiding. He looks to us as if he is in fancy dress, with his hair powdered white in the fashion of the time, but at that time all children were made to wear exact copies of grown-up clothes. His face is very solemn; few portraits of Wolfgang ever showed his mischievous nature.

In the June of that year, 1763, when Wolfgang was seven and Nannerl twelve, the whole family set out on their first Grand Tour—a tour that was going to last nearly three and a half years, and take them all over Europe. Leopold had leave of absence from Archbishop Schrattenbach, who, with an easy-going generosity typical of him, paid him a retaining salary and kept his job for him while he was away. This was fairly common practice in Germany and Austria then, as musicians were expected to travel.

This time they went in their own carriage with a servant. On

Facsimile of the manuscript of the Andante for piano, K.9b, written by Mozart in Salzburg in 1763 at the age of seven

the first day a back wheel broke and they had to stop for days in a little town called Wasserburg while it was mended. Leopold took Wolfgang into the church, which had a good organ.

Wolfgang had not yet learned to play the pedal organ properly and was apparently fascinated by it. At that time, though the organ was an ancient instrument, it was still in the process of being developed; many instruments had only manuals (keyboards) and no pedals. The organ at Wasserburg was presumably a big one, of the sort Bach composed on; to

The organ of Salzburg Cathedral. A photograph

Wolfgang it was a new challenge. He watched his father demonstrate how to play the pedals. In a letter to Hagenauer, 21 June 1763, Leopold takes up the story:

The latest news is that in order to amuse ourselves we went to the organ and I explained to Woferl the use of the pedal. Whereupon he tried it *stante pede,* shoved the stool away and played standing at the organ, at the same time working the pedal, and doing it all as if he had been practising it for several months. Everyone was amazed. Indeed this is a fresh act of God's grace, which many a one only receives after much labours.

The family travelled on through Germany—to Munich, Mannheim, Augsburg, Heidelberg, Frankfurt. In her tavel diary Nannerl left some recollections of the trip:

In Munich I saw the Nymphenburg palace and the garden and the four castles, namely Amalienburg, Badenburg, Bagodenburg, and the Eremitage. Amalienburg is the most beautiful, it has a fine bed and the little kitchen where the Elector's consort herself did the cooking. Badenburg is the biggest, there is a hall all of mirrors and the bath is marble. Bagodenburg is the smallest, the walls are of majolica. And the Eremitage is the most decorous.

Leopold had by now worked out a plan, so that his children had at least some advance publicity. Before the Mozart's arrival a newspaper in Augsburg published this:

... The greatest wonder in all Germany. ... Imagine if you can a girl of eleven years who plays the most difficult sonatas and concertos ... with the most distinct execution, with almost incredible ease, and in the best taste. That alone would be enough to astonish many people. But we are transported with utter amazement when we see a boy of six years sitting at a harpsichord, and hear him not only playing the same sonatas, trios and concertos manfully, not at all like a child, but also hear him improvising from his head, for whole hours at a time, or reading at sight to accompany symphonies, arias, and recitatives at concerts.
I have moreover seen the keyboard covered for him with a cloth, and he played as well as if he had the keys before his eyes.
I have moreover seen and heard when he was placed in another room and single notes were played, not only on the clavier, but on any other instrument, and in the very instant he named the letter or name of the given note. Indeed, when he heard a bell peal or a clock, or even a pocket watch, he could name its tone at once.
Given a few notes of a melody, he would reproduce it and then put the bass to it himself, which he did each time so beautifully, precisely and excellently that all were wonderstruck.

29

There was much more to the *avertissement*.

Every side of music came to Wolfgang as easily as eating or
sleeping. He needed almost no teaching; it seemed he knew
everything already.

They left Germany, and started driving through the Austrian
Netherlands, getting nearer to Paris, their main destination,
every day. But because of rough, bad roads, their carriage
broke down again, and they found themselves stuck in a little
Dutch village. Leopold describes their inn, giving a vivid
picture of ordinary life in Holland in those days.

We sat down on Dutch wicker chairs by the fireplace, where a
cauldron hung from a long chain, holding meat, turnips and all sorts
of other things boiling away together. We were given a miserable
little tablecloth, and soup and fish were served to us, along with a
bottle of red champagne. The door was left open constantly so that
we frequently had the honour of a visit from the pigs, who grunted all
around us.

On 18 November 1763 the Mozarts reached Paris. A new
stage in Wolfgang's career had begun, in a big busy city which
regarded the rest of the world as provincial.

Mozart and his sister about 1763

Leopold Mozart, about 1763

Paris in the eighteenth century

Chapter 3

Paris and London

'As an artist, or a musician, Mozart was not a man of this world'—Alfred Einstein

Paris was a gay, sophisticated, bewildering city, a city of contrasts, of very rich and very poor, and when the Mozarts first arrived they felt rather lost and nervous. Fortunately, Leopold had organised his usual letters of introduction to important people, and he soon found influential friends to help launch his children into the Parisian musical scene.

Their greatest friend, and the person who did most for them in their five months in Paris, was a man called Melchior Grimm, who was a leading intellectual figure. When he first heard Wolfgang play he was astounded. But what really impressed him was the boy's *creative* abilities.

He was so impressed in fact that he published the following notice in the *Correspondance littéraire* for 11 December 1763, just twelve days after the Mozarts had arrived in Paris:

True miracles are so rare that it behoves us to report one when it comes our way. A *Kapellmeister* of Salzburg named Mozart has just arrived here with two children who present the prettiest appearance in the world. His daughter, eleven years of age, plays the clavier in the most brilliant manner, executing the longest and most difficult pieces with amazing precision. Her brother, who will be seven years old next February [*sic*], is so extraordinary a phenomenon that we can scarcely credit what we see with our own eyes and hear with our own ears. Easily and with utmost accuracy, the child performs the most difficult pieces with hands that are scarcely large enough to span a sixth. It is a wondrous thing to see him improvising for a whole hour, giving himself entirely to the inspiration of his genius and generating a host of delightful musical ideas, which, moreover, he unfolds successively with admirable taste and excellent clarity. The finest conductor has not so deep a knowledge of harmony and modulation,

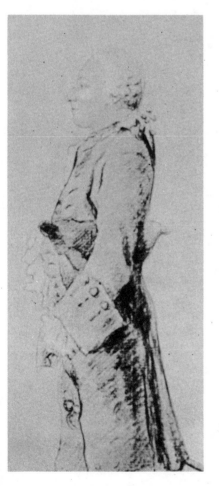

31

Leopold Mozart with Wolfgang and Nannerl in Paris. Watercolour by Carmontelle, 1763. Delafosse subsequently made an engraving of this picture which was then used as the basis for an advertisement distributed throughout Europe (Musée Condé, Chantilly)

which this child applies in unusual but always correct ways. Such is his adeptness on the keyboard that if it is covered with a napkin he continues to play through the napkin with the same speed and precision. He has not the slightest difficulty deciphering anything that is put before him; he writes and composes with wonderful ease, without the necessity of repairing to the clavier to pick out his accords. I wrote out a minuet for him with my own hands, and asked him to put a bass to it; the child took the pen and without repairing to the clavier straightway wrote the bass below my minuet.

You can well imagine that it costs him not the slightest effort to transpose any aria placed before him out of any key into any other, and to play it. But the following incident, which I witnessed, eludes explanation. A lady asked him casually whether he would accompany her by ear, and without looking at her, in an Italian *cavatina* that she knew by heart. She began to sing; the child tried a bass which was formally correct, in so far as it is impossible to give in advance the accompaniment of a song one does not know. But as soon as the song was over he asked the lady to begin again from the beginning, and this time he not only played the entire melody with the right hand, but at the same time added the bass with his left without the slightest uncertainty. Then he requested her ten times in succession to begin again, and with each repetition he changed the character of his accompaniment. He would have gone through it twenty times more had he not been asked to stop. It is evident that this child will end by turning my head completely if I hear him more often. I now understand the overwhelming effect of miracles. I am no longer astonished that St. Paul's reason was shaken after his strange vision. Mozart's children have aroused the admiration and wonder of all who have seen them. The Emperor and Empress have lavished kindness upon them, and they have enjoyed a similar reception at the courts of Munich and Mannheim. It is a pity that in this country music is so little understood! The father intends to proceed from here to England, and then to take his children back home by way of North Germany.

Wolfgang's small concerts in Paris interested the smart, rich nobility, but so far they did little more than discuss him. Leopold realised that, as usual, until the King had commanded a concert, the nobility would not invite the Mozarts to their houses. The etiquette was the same throughout Europe;

Versailles, the palace and gardens

33

musicians, and other artists of all sorts, knew they would get nowhere until they had been noticed by the leader of court life, be it king, emperor or lord. As Wolfgang Mozart grew up, he was to hate this need to crawl before the great more and more, although he knew it was an established part of the world he lived in.

So just before Christmas, the whole family moved to Versailles; here since the reign of the Roi Soleil, Louis XIV, was the official court of the French kings, in the vast and grandiose Palace of Versailles. On Christmas Eve the Mozarts heard Mass in the Royal Chapel: Wolfgang was fascinated by the different style of choral music. He was learning something new every day.

At last, on New Year's Day, came the Royal summons; the Mozarts were invited to a public court dinner. They went, dressed in new black finery, and were placed near King Louis XV's table. The Royal family made a great fuss of Wolfgang and Nannerl, to the surprise of the haughty French aristocracy. Later Wolfgang played the organ in front of the whole court, with the applause of all. It is surprising that all the praise and attention given him when he was young never made him at all vain or arrogant.

Leopold has given us a vivid account of this particular evening in a letter of 1 February 1764 addressed to Hagenauer's wife:

Since my last letter from Versailles I would assuredly have written to you, only I kept on postponing this in order to await the result of our affair at Versailles and be able to tell you about it. But as everything here, even more so than at other courts, goes at a snail's pace, . . . one must be patient. If the recognition we receive equals the pleasure which my children have given this court, we ought to do very well. I should like to tell you that it is not the custom here to kiss the hand of royal persons or to disturb them with a petition or even to speak to them *au passage,* as they call it, that is to say, when they walk to church through the gallery and the royal apartments. Neither is it the custom here to do homage either by an inclination of the head or a genuflexion to the King or to members of the Royal Family. On the contrary, one remains erect and immovable, and, standing thus, one just lets the King and his family pass close by. Hence you can well imagine how impressed and amazed these French people, who are so infatuated with their court customs, must have been, when the King's daughters, not only in their apartments but in the public gallery, stopped when they saw my children, came up to them and not only allowed them to kiss their hands, but kissed them innumerable times. And the same thing happened with Madame la Dauphine. But what appeared most extraordinary to these French people was that at the.

Detail of the illustration below showing Mozart at the clavier

Mozart playing at a musical tea at the Prince de Conti's, 1764

Marie Leszcynska, Queen of France

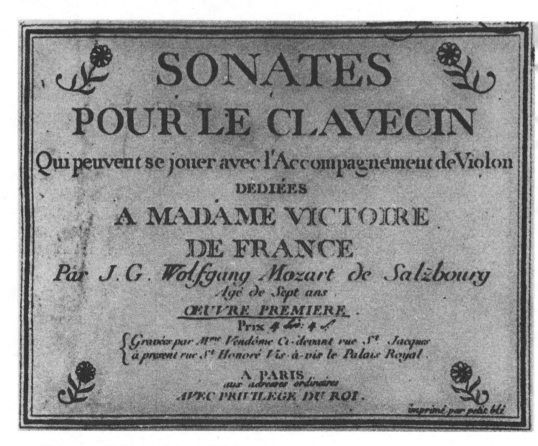

Title page of Mozart's first published work

grand couvert on the evening of New Year's Day, not only was it necessary to make room for us all to go up to the royal table, but my Wolfgang was graciously privileged to stand beside the Queen the whole time, to talk constantly to her, entertain her and kiss her hands repeatedly, besides partaking of the dishes which she handed him from the table. The Queen speaks as good German as we do and, as the King knows none, she interpreted to him everything that our gallant Wolfgang said. I stood beside him, and on the other side of the King, where M. le Dauphin and Madame Adélaïde were seated,

Louis XV (1710–74).
Portrait by
Louis–Michel Vanloo
(Grenoble Museum)

stood my wife and daughter. Now you must know that the King never dines in public, except on Sunday evenings when the whole Royal Family dine together. But not everyone is allowed to be present. When, however, there is a great festival, such as New Year's Day, Easter, Whitsuntide, the name-days and so forth, the *grand couvert* is held, to which all persons of distinction are admitted. There is not, however, very much room and consequently the hall soon gets filled up. We arrived late. So the Swiss Guards had to make way for us and we were led through the hall into the room close to the royal table, through which the Royal Family enter. As they passed us they spoke to our Wolfgang and we then followed them to table.

Now all the French nobles invited Wolfgang to give concerts at their houses. He met all the other court musicians, well-known composers, pianists, violinists, cellists; there were also troupes of singers, actors and dancers. It was a stimulating time.

The Mozarts returned from Versailles to Paris, all doors open to them. But just at this point Wolfgang fell ill again, with a bad throat infection, and had to stay indoors. He probably had a rather miserable eighth birthday in bed.

As soon as he was better a big public concert was organised, which took place on 10 March. It was a success, and to Leopold's joy they made a lot of money. Often concerts were applauded, but made no money; there would just be praise and presents. The presents were often very beautiful—jewels, watches, swords, gold snuff-boxes, clothes—but they did not buy food unless you pawned them, as Leopold said bitterly.

It was in Paris that Wolfgang Mozart's compositions first appeared in print: four sonatas for clavier and violin, two of which Wolfgang had composed in Paris. Leopold was almost more excited about it than Wolfgang, and wrote gloatingly in a letter: 'Picture to yourself the furore which the music will make in the world when people read on the title-page that it has been composed by a seven-year-old child.'

Wolfgang gave another big and very successful concert in Paris (on 9 April), and the very next day, before their luck could turn, as it always seemed to if they stayed too long in a place, they left Paris. Now they were going on to conquer London.

None of the family had ever seen the sea before. They stayed in Calais for three days getting used to its strangeness; Leopold hired a boat rather than taking the usual mail-boat (which was then called the 'packet'), and when they finally made the crossing they were all sea-sick. A horde of rude porters descended on them at Dover and made Leopold very angry;

the stage-coach from Dover to London was crowded, and the road bad, sometimes no better than a cart-track. There was also the fear of footpads, or highwaymen, attacking the coach.

Then, suddenly, they could see the spires of London, and in no time they were joining the queue of coaches moving slowly across old London Bridge. Beneath them the Thames was

London and the Thames in 1750

The great Florentine castrato, Giovanni Manzuoli (1725–80). Engraving by G. B. Betti after the portrait by Luigi Betti

packed with ships and boats of all descriptions: the river then was London's main highway. The date was 23 April 1764.

London was a very rich city—not just with a rich nobility, as in Paris, but with rich merchants and traders as well. Great Britain drew wealth from all her new colonies—India, Canada, the American Colonies, the West and East Indies. Fabulous riches poured into the City of London, brought by sailing ships from all over the world. In the fifteen months the Mozarts spent in London they earned larger sums of money than they ever had before.

London was a centre of music, more so than Paris; George III and Queen Charlotte loved music, and encouraged every side of it. They went to many concerts themselves, and to the opera once a week.

George Frederick Handel, after dominating the musical scene for forty-five years, had died only five years before Mozart arrived in London. He had been the favourite court composer, and his music was still being widely performed.

Then there was Johann Christian Bach, the great Johann Sebastian Bach's son. J. C. Bach was the Queen's music master, and mainly composed, like Handel, operas in Italian.

St. James's Park and
Buckingham House,
London. An engraving,
1763

But he also wrote symphonies and concertos, all of which were
to be remembered by Wolfgang.

Italian opera was almost a passion with Londoners of the
eighteenth century, and Wolfgang was excited to find so many
first-rate Italian singers in one city. Different operas were
performed every day, and the Mozarts went to as many as they
could.

Wolfgang's one main desire now was to compose an Italian
opera; he thought about it night and day. He met the greatest
singer in London, the castrato, Manzuoli; in no time they were
the best of friends, Manzuoli giving Wolfgang singing lessons,
and in return Wolfgang writing arias for him.

Within five days of their first arrival in London the Mozarts
were summoned to court by the music-loving King and Queen.
They went to St. James's in their new English clothes; fashions
were quite different in London from those in Paris.

They were given a splendid welcome, 'exceeding all others',
wrote Leopold. Wolfgang played all the King's favourite works
by Bach and Handel at sight; he played the King's organ

38

'The Inside View of the Rotunda in Ranelagh Gardens, with the Company at Breakfast'. An engraving, 1754. 'You cannot conceive what a sweet elegant delicious place [it] is. Paradise itself can hardly be equal to it', observed Mrs. Ellison in Henry Fielding's novel *The History of Amelia* (1751)

beautifully, and accompanied the Queen in an aria which she sang. George III and Queen Charlotte were astounded, and introduced the eight-year-old boy at once to the court composer, Johann Christian Bach. He and Wolfgang liked each other immediately on sight, and admired one another's music. The younger Bach had a great influence from then onwards on Wolfgang's early compositions.

In June, two months after their arrival, Wolfgang and Nannerl gave their first big public concert. Golden guineas and praise poured in: it was probably the most successful concert they had so far given anywhere. Performing with the two children were four Italian opera singers, who sang arias written by Wolfgang. The whole of London buzzed about the child genius. Beside his performances at public concerts, each day between twelve noon and two o'clock he and the rest of the family were at home in their rooms in Soho for anyone who cared to come along and prove for himself that this boy-miracle of eight years old was not just a fairy-story.

At the end of June (on the 29th) Wolfgang appeared at a charity concert held in the rotunda of Ranelagh Gardens, one of the renowned pleasure gardens of eighteenth century London down by the river. He played an organ concerto and also some of his own keyboard pieces on the harpsichord. The *Public Advertiser* announced him as 'the most extraordinary prodigy and most amazing genius that has appeared in any age'.

During the summer Leopold was very ill, and for seven weeks the family moved into the country to recuperate. The 'country' was Chelsea, then a little village two miles from London. When we read Leopold's letter describing Chelsea we can see how much London has changed in two hundred years. The Mozarts rented a house with a large, lovely garden: 'It has one of the most beautiful views in the world,' wrote Leopold. 'Wherever I turn my eyes, I only see gardens and in the distance the finest castles.'

A month or so later, on 13 September, Leopold wrote again to Hagenauer:

I now state that every day, although my progress is slow, I am feeling a little better, so that I am confident that I have no internal disorder. So that you may know, however, how my illness started, I must tell you that in England there is a kind of native complaint, which is called a *'cold'*. That is why you hardly ever see people wearing summer clothes. They all wear cloth garments. This so-called *'cold'* in the case of people who are not constitutionally sound, becomes so dangerous that in many cases it develops into a *'consumption'* as they call it here; but I call it *'febrem lentam'*; and the wisest course for such people to adopt is to leave England and cross the sea; and many instances can be found of people recovering their health on leaving this country.

Wolfgang loved these seven quiet weeks in Chelsea. He and Nannerl were not allowed to touch the clavier in case it disturbed his father, and so he spent his time composing and learning from the example of Christian Bach.

'Do you know,' Wolfgang is reputed to have said to Nannerl, 'I think Johann Christian Bach is by far the nicest man I've ever met. I'm composing a symphony in the style he uses.' This was Wolfgang's first symphony (E flat major, K.16) and whenever Bach came to see them he told him how it was going.

One of the most important things Bach also taught Wolfgang was the Italian 'singing allegro', and you will find the clear, gay spirit of this in all Mozart's music throughout his life.

His improvisation sessions with Bach became famous. Grimm tells also how Bach would take the young boy on his

Two views of Chelsea

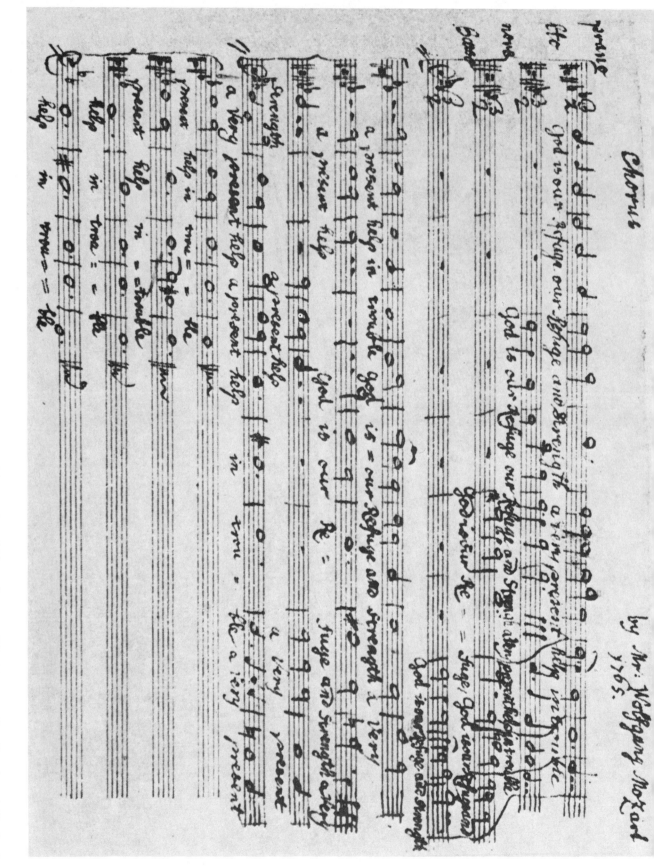

Manuscript of Mozart's motet "God is our refuge," written in England

knees, and in this way they played together, alternating on the same clavier, for two hours without interruption, in the presence of the King and Queen.

While he was in Chelsea Wolfgang composed a further symphony and other pieces in an album that has since become known as the 'Chelsea Notebook'. Since he had left Salzburg a year before, his development had been so rapid that his friends at home would hardly have believed it. Many musicians in London now became jealous of him, and rumours went round that he was much older than he looked. An Englishman called Daines Barrington, who was a distinguished lawyer and historian as well as musician, decided he would clear up the problem of Wolfgang's age himself. He invited him to his house and put him through all sorts of difficult tests; these he

Johann Christian Bach
(1735–82). One of two
portraits by Thomas
Gainsborough

The 1764 'Chelsea Notebook'. A facsimile of bars 18–36 of the thirty-fourth piece. The manuscript, originally in the Preussische Staatsbibliothek, Berlin, has been lost since the Second World War

then wrote up for an address delivered to the Royal Society in 1770.

As during this time I was witness of his most extraordinary abilities as a musician, both at some publick concerts, and likewise by having been alone with him for a considerable time at his father's house; I send you the following account, amazing and incredible almost as it may appear.

I carried to him a manuscript duet, which was composed by an English gentleman to some favourite words in Metastasio's opera of Demofoönte.

The whole score was in five parts, viz. accompaniments for a first and second violin, the two vocal parts, and a base.

I shall here likewise mention, that the parts for the first and second voice were written in what the Italians *stile* the *Contralto* cleff; the reason for taking notice of which particular will appear hereafter. . . .

The score was no sooner put upon his desk, than he began to play the symphony in a most masterly manner, as well as in the time and *stile* which correspond with the intention of the composer. . . .

42

The symphony ended, he took the upper part, leaving the under one to his father.

His voice in the tone of it was thin and infantine, but nothing could exceed the masterly manner in which he sung.

His father, who took the under part in this duet, was once or twice out, though the passages were not more difficult than those in the upper one; on which occasions the son looked back with some anger, pointing out to him his mistakes, and setting him right.

He not only however did complete justice to the duet, by singing his own part in the truest taste, and with the greatest precision: he also threw in the accompaniments of the two violins, wherever they were most necessary, and produced the best effects. . . .

When he had finished the duet, he expressed himself highly in its approbation, asking with some eagerness whether I had brought any more such music.

Having been informed, however, that he was often visited with musical ideas, to which, even in the midst of the night, he would give utterance on his harpsichord, I told his father that I should be glad to hear some of his extemporary compositions.

The father shook his head at this, saying that it depended entirely upon his being as it were musically inspired, but that I might ask him whether he was in humour for such a composition.

Happening to know that little Mozart was much taken notice of by Manzoli [sic], the famous singer, who came over to England in 1764, I said to the boy, that I should be glad to hear an extemporary *Love Song,* such as his friend Manzoli [sic] might choose in an opera.

The boy on this (who continued to sit at his harpsichord) looked back with much archness, and immediately began five or six lines of a jargon recitative proper to introduce a love song.

He then played a symphony which might correspond with an air composed to the single word, *Affetto.*

It had a first and second part, which together with the symphonies, was of the length that opera songs generally last: if this extemporary composition was not amazingly capital, yet it was really above mediocrity, and shewed most extraordinary readiness of invention.

Finding that he was in humour, and as it were inspired, I then desired him to compose a *Song of Rage,* such as might be proper for the opera stage.

The boy again looked back with much archness, and began five or six lines of a jargon recitative proper to precede a *Song of Anger.*

This lasted also about the same time with the *Song of Love;* and in the middle of it, he had worked himself up to such a pitch, that he beat his harpsichord like a person possessed, rising sometimes in his chair.

The word he pitched upon for this second extemporary composition was *Perfido.*

After this he played a difficult lesson, which he had finished a day or two before: his execution was amazing, considering that his little fingers could scarcely reach a fifth on the harpsichord.

Queen Charlotte of England (1744–1818). She married George III in 1761 and bore him fifteen children

His astonishing readiness, however, did not arise merely from great practice; he had a thorough knowledge of the fundamental principles of composition, as, upon producing a treble, he immediately wrote a base under it, which, when tried, had a very good effect.

He was also a great master of modulation, and his transitions from one key to another were excessively natural and judicious; he practised in this manner for a considerable time with an handkerchief over the keys of the harpsichord.

The facts which I have been mentioning I was myself an eye witness of; to which I must add, that I have been informed by two or three able musicians, when [Johann Christian] Bach the celebrated composer had begun a fugue and left off abruptly, that little Mozart hath immediately taken it up, and worked it after a most masterly manner.

Witness as I was myself of most of these extraordinary facts, I must own that I could not help suspecting his father imposed with regard to the real age of the boy, though he had not only a most childish appearance, but likewise had all the actions of that stage of life.

For example, whilst he was playing to me, a favourite cat came in, upon which he immediately left his harpsichord, nor could we bring him back for a considerable time.

He would also sometimes run about the room with a stick between his legs by way of horse.

I found likewise that most of the London musicians were of the same opinion with regard to his age, not believing it possible that a child of so tender years could surpass most of the masters in that science.

I have therefore for a considerable time made the best inquiries I was able from some of the German musicians resident in London, but could never receive any further information than that he was born near Salsbourg [sic], till I was so fortunate as to procure an extract from the register of that place, through his excellence count Haslang.

It appears from this extract, that Mozart's father did not impose with regard to his age when he was in England, for it was in June, 1765, that I was witness to what I have above related, when the boy was only eight [actually nine] years and five months old.

That winter of his ninth birthday (1764/65) Wolfgang wrote and published six sonatas for violin and harpsichord dedicated to Queen Charlotte who sent him a princely sum of fifty guineas. He had been in England over a year now, and Londoners had got used to the prodigy in their midst. The Mozarts' income became smaller. They moved from the elegant but expensive West End into the City, and began giving daily performances in a tavern called The Swan and Hoop. Leopold invented a new trick for his children to do: they both played at one and the same clavier, covering the keyboard with a cloth. For these performances Wolfgang com-

King George III of England (1737-1820)

Title page of the sonatas
dedicated to Queen Charlotte

Six
SONATES
pour le
CLAVECIN
qui peuvent se jouer avec
L'accompagnement de Violon ou Flaute
Traversiere
Très humblement dediées
A SA MAJESTÉ
CHARLOTTE
REINE de la GRANDE BRETAGNE
Composées par
I.G. WOLFGANG MOZART
Agé de huit Ans
Oeuvre III.

LONDON Printed for the Author and Sold at his Lodging
At Mr. Williamson in Thrift Street Soho

Mozart by John Zoffany, about 1765

posed special four-hand clavier sonatas—almost the first pieces of this type in the world. Leopold burst with pride.

Wolfgang was extremely happy in London, and had not fallen ill once. He had seen all the sights: Westminster Abbey, St. Paul's, the Royal Exchange, the gardens at Vauxhall, the British Museum and of course, the Tower where, Leopold tells us, the roaring of the lions frightened him. He was heartbroken when in July Leopold decided they must leave England. What upset him most of all, however, was saying good-bye to Johann Christian Bach; he never forgot Bach, and all his life he loved him more than any other composer he ever met. At the end of his life London was still the place which attracted him most, and to which he hoped and planned to return. He never did.

Leopold Mozart. Anonymous portrait, c. 1765 (Salzburg Mozarteum)

Chapter 4

The First Opera

'I like an aria to fit a singer as perfectly as a well-tailored suit of clothes'—Mozart

As soon as the Mozart family arrived in France, Wolfgang fell ill. Then Leopold fell ill. When they were better they went to the Hague in Holland to give a series of concerts. Two days after they arrived Nannerl fell ill; and this time it was very serious. Her fever grew worse; she became so thin she was just skin and bones. Then she became delirious, and talked wildly in all the languages she knew—French, Italian and English. This sounded so funny that the family could not help laughing a little in spite of their worry. It was the only thing that cheered Wolfgang up, though not for very long, because everyone expected Nannerl to die.

Miraculously, she got better. Then, of course, Wolfgang

The residence of the Stadtholder in The Hague. An engraving

caught the same disease, and because his resistance was much lower, it hit him even harder. He very nearly died. His mother and father were frantic with worry; they sent for the best doctors available and, slowly, Wolfgang recovered. He was quite unrecognisable he was so thin.

Probably the disease that nearly killed the two children was typhus; doctors in those days knew very little about disease and medicine, and sometimes when one reads their prescriptions one is not at all surprised that their patients really did die.

After a delay of several months Wolfgang and Nannerl eventually gave a few highly acclaimed concerts at the Dutch Court, and in the March of 1766 contributed to the installation of the Prince of Orange as *Stadtholder*. Then in the spring when the weather was better again they travelled back to Paris. They had left a variety of things behind before going to London, which Leopold now wanted to collect. All their Parisian friends found that both children had grown and changed immensely in two years, particularly Wolfgang, who was now ten. Melchior Grimm, their old friend, was especially impressed by Wolfgang's musical development, above all in composition. Grimm was perceptive enough to realise that it was in this, not in performing on instruments, that the boy's true genius lay. It was Grimm who prophesied that Wolfgang's goal as a composer must be Italian opera.

Grimm described the Mozart's second visit in the *Correspondance littéraire:*

Mademoiselle Mozart, now thirteen years old, who has incidentally grown very pretty, plays the clavier in the finest and most brilliant manner imaginable; her brother alone can rob her of applause. This remarkable boy is now nine years old. He has scarcely grown physically, but has made wonderful progress in music.

He has even written several Italian arias, and I do not abandon the hope that before he is twelve years old he will already have an opera performed in some Italian theatre. In London he heard Manzuoli for an entire winter, and profited so well by this experience that although his own voice is feeble he sings with good taste and feeling. But most incomprehensible of all is the profound knowledge of harmony and its most secret resources which he possesses to such an extreme degree.

Famous musicians in Paris wanted to compete with Wolfgang in what they called musical contests. Grimm describes what happened:

We have seen him pitted in contests for an hour and a half at a stretch with musicians who had perspiration streaming from their

Mozart aged thirteen.
Portrait by Thaddeus
Helbling, 1767 (Oxford
University Press)

brows as they strained every nerve to keep up with a boy who himself left the scene of the struggle with no sign of weariness. I have seen him at the organ confounding and silencing organists who thought themselves extremely skilful. In London, Bach took him on his knees, and in this way they played together, alternating on the same clavier, for two hours without interruption in the presence of the King and Queen. . . . One might go on talking endlessly about this unique phenomenon.

Grimm also tells us what Wolfgang was like:

He is one of the most charming lads imaginable: there is wit and feeling in everything he says and does, united with the grace and charm of his age. In fact, his liveliness relieves one of the fear that so premature a fruit might fall before it is ripe.

In other words, Grimm had no fear that Wolfgang would not go on developing as he grew older. His naturalness, sense of fun and lovableness impressed everybody; so did his wide general knowledge of things outside music, and his ability to speak excellent French, Italian and English besides German. With all these accomplishments he was still exceptionally modest, and did not care a jot about praise. Yet for all his independent liveliness, he was utterly obedient to his parents; he worshipped his father's clear-cut ideas and energy, and found peaceful companionship in his mother's kind and solid goodness. In fact, if anything, he was altogether too dependent on them, so that when later he began to live on his own, his lack of training made him impractical and chaotic about business affairs.

Soon the Mozarts were on the road again, and after a slow journey, stopping to give concerts at many cities, including Geneva and Lausanne, they reached Salzburg on the last day of November 1766, after being away for three and a half exciting and successful years. Wolfgang was world-famous, aged ten.

Returning to Salzburg was like returning to prison. The Salzburgers were as narrow-minded and unappreciative as ever, except for the Archbishop, who continued to be kind and generous. He had, of course, been paying Leopold a salary all the time he had been away. The rest of the nobility took no notice of the Mozarts at all.

Salzburg. An engraving by Mozart's contemporary, Franz von Neumann

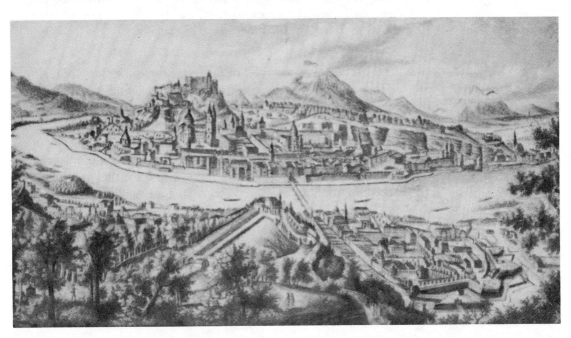

The situation Wolfgang experienced at this time has been well described by Erich Schenk in his book, *Mozart and His Times:*

As one result of personal intercourse with Europe's foremost musicians, his [Leopold's] child prodigy, who had displayed such amazing musicality and virtuosity at the time of his departure, had matured into a composer of astonishing ability. Musical competitions had strengthened the boy's self-confidence. One indication of this was the haughty retorts he gave to prominent citizens of Salzburg who spoke patronizingly to this world-famous boy.

He and his family had associated with the foremost personages of Europe, and had been treated by them as equals, not as members of the socially disdained class of musicians. Here lay the germ of Wolfgang's tragic conflict with the society of his time, once the miracle of his being a prodigy ended. Here, too, we may see the origin of that sense of superiority which the far-travelled young man felt toward the narrow environment of Salzburg. His untrammelled expression of such sentiments made him appear supercilious as a boy and young man, although he never behaved with arrogance toward the members of his own family, as did many far less important child prodigies. One of the most engaging traits of Mozart in boyhood was, in fact, this charm of a child who obeyed his parents' wishes fully and joyously.

It seems not to have occurred to Leopold Mozart [however] that the boy's triumphs had been achieved at the expense of severe damage to his health. He overlooked the fact that Wolfgang's physical development had not kept pace, could not keep pace, with his intellectual progress. He ignored the boy's nervous fits of weeping caused by homesickness or by the news that his childhood friend Dominicus Hagenauer had entered a monastery.

The Mozarts only stayed in Salzburg for ten months. During this time Wolfgang was composing and studying music busily, as well as having lessons in other subjects—arithmetic, history, Latin. He composed arias, sonatas, an operetta and some church music. He was also asked to write the first act of an oratorio. Other musicians in Salzburg were envious, and spread the rumour that someone helped him. So the story goes (according to Daines Barrington) that he was shut up for a week in the Archbishop's palace, where in strict confinement he wrote a very fine oratorio, amazed everybody and silenced his critics.

There was one thing Wolfgang had not done yet: he had not written an Italian opera. Leopold decided to take him to Vienna again, the nearest place where new operas were commissioned and performed. There was another good reason

Vienna, the Lobkowitz Palace, residence of one of the great Viennese patrons of music. Painting by Bernardo Bellotto, a nephew of Canaletto, *c.* 1760

for going to Vienna: one of Empress Maria Theresia's daughters, Maria Josepha, was being married to the King of Naples, and new music would be needed for the festivities at court.

But this time Vienna did not open all its doors to the Mozarts. Etiquette demanded, as usual, that no concerts could be given until one was given at court. But the court was in a turmoil because young Maria Josepha had caught the dreaded smallpox; and in the middle of October she died. All festivities ceased at once, and the fear of smallpox drove everyone from Vienna.

Leopold took his family away quickly, but it was too late—Wolfgang had already caught smallpox. He was very ill, but fortunately a good doctor and a naturally strong constitution helped him survive a disease that most people died of. Nannerl also caught it, but not so badly.

By Wolfgang's twelfth birthday in January they went back to Vienna, and things were better. The Imperial family summoned them to court, and remembering their visit of nearly six years earlier, were very kind to them. The Emperor himself, Joseph II (Francis I had died in 1765 and his son had succeeded to the throne), suggested that Wolfgang should write an Italian opera:

Can you not imagine [Leopold wrote] what a turmoil secretly arose amongst those composers? What? Today we are to see a Gluck and tomorrow a boy of twelve seated at the harpsichord and conducting

Joseph II, right, and his brother (later Leopold II) as young men. Detail from a painting by Pompeo Batoni (Vienna Kunsthistorisches Museum)

his own opera? Yes, despite all those who envy him! I have even won Gluck over to our side, though, I admit, only to the extent that, though he is not quite whole-hearted, he has decided not to let it be noticed; for our patrons are his also. In order to make our position safe in regard to the actors, who usually cause the composer most annoyance, I have taken the matter up with them, and one of them has given me all the suggestions for the work. But, in reality it was the Emperor himself who first gave me the idea of getting little Wolfgang to write an opera. For he asked the boy twice whether he would like to compose an opera and conduct it himself? Wolfgang said, Yes. But more than this the Emperor could not suggest . . . The consequences of this undertaking, if God helps us to carry it out, are so enormous, but so easy to visualize, that they require no explanation. But now I must spare no money, for it will come back to me today or tomorrow. Never venture, never win. I must show what we can do. We must succeed or fail. And where is my boy more likely to succeed than in the theatre?

The opera was called *La Finta Semplice* (*The Simple Pretence*) and Wolfgang worked hard on it. By July it was finished. But as usual jealous musicians said a boy of twelve could not possibly write an opera alone.

In a bitter letter to Hagenauer (30 July 1768), Leopold illuminated the problems:

At first the opera was to be performed at Easter. But the poet [Marco Coltellini] was the first to prevent this, for, on the pretext of making here and there certain necessary alterations, he kept on delaying, so that by Easter we had received from him only two of the amended arias. Next, the opera was fixed for Whitsuntide and then for the return of His Majesty from Hungary. But at this point the mask fell from the face. For in the meantime all the composers, amongst whom Gluck is a leading figure, undermined everything in order to prevent the success of this opera. The singers were talked over, the orchestra were worked up and every means was used to stop its performance. The singers who, moreover, hardly know their parts and one or two of whom have to learn everything entirely by ear, were now put up to say that they could not sing their arias, which they had nevertheless previously heard in our room and which they had approved of, applauded and described as quite suitable for them. The orchestra were now to say that they did not like a boy to conduct them, and a hundred similar things. Meanwhile some people spread the report that the music was not worth a fig; others said that it did not fit the words, or was àgainst the metre, thus proving that the boy had not sufficient command of the Italian language. As soon as I heard this, I made it quite clear in the most eminent quarters that Hasse, the father of music, and the great Metastasio had stated that the slanderers who spread this report should go to them and hear out of their own mouths that thirty operas have been performed in Vienna, which in no respect can touch this boy's opera which they both admire in the very highest degree. Then it was said that not the boy, but his father had written it. But here too the credit of the slanderers began to fall. For they dropped *ab uno extremo ad aliud* until they were in the soup. I asked someone to take any portion of the works of Metastasio, open the book and put before little Wolfgang the first aria which he should hit upon. Wolfgang took up his pen and with the most amazing rapidity wrote, without hesitation and in the presence of several eminent persons, the music for this aria for several instruments.

The feat silenced the critics.

Yet the fuss and intrigue behind the scenes at the court opera house continued: and so many people sided against Mozart that in the end he and his father gave up the unequal struggle. The opera was cancelled. They felt sad and bitter. Wolfgang had worked on his opera until he was exhausted; he had written 558 pages of music in composing it. But he did not let this setback depress him too much, and went on composing—a little operetta, two Masses, sonatas and a symphony.

While they were in Vienna his father made a list of all Wolfgang's compositions; there were well over eighty, of which fifty are still in existence; the others are lost. These include six symphonies, thirteen Italian arias, and a *Stabat mater.*

When the family returned to Salzburg in January 1769, just

The Rennweg Orphanage in Vienna. According to Leopold, Mozart wrote some music for the orphanage choir in 1768, including a Mass and a trumpet concerto. Fragments of the Mass have come to light since the Second World War

before Wolfgang's thirteenth birthday, the Archbishop arranged that the opera *La Finta Semplice* should be properly performed in Salzburg on 1 May, the sovereign's name-day. It was a great success, and made up for the disappointments of Vienna.

The Mozarts stayed in Salzburg for eleven months, and Wolfgang had a well-earned rest. One thing he could never stop doing, however, and that was composing. There was nothing much else to do in Salzburg anyway, and the busier he became the less annoyed he was by his fellow citizens.

By the end of that year he felt strong, rested and ready for anything. He and Leopold now were going to do something they had thought about for years: they were going to Italy. Italy at last, the home of opera. Wolfgang was happy and confident; he had grown up a lot in the last year and now, nearly fourteen, he was ready to face the highly critical Italian audiences. He was no longer little Wolfgang, the boy prodigy; he was Mozart, a young composer and performer with a brilliant future ahead of him. He knew now his genius was not just a childhood flash in the pan: it was something great and lasting.

He and his father left for Italy in early December 1769. They left his mother, Anna-Maria Mozart, and Nannerl behind them. One of Mozart's first letters to his mother (13 December) shows how happy he was.

I am utterly delighted, in sheer pleasure, because it is so much fun on this trip, because it is so warm in the carriage, and because our coachman is a gay fellow who drives so fast whenever the road gives him any chance at all.

The new adventure was beginning well.

Chapter 5

Italy

'He can say very much, but he never says too much'—Busoni

Verona, the theatre

Italy in those days was not a united independent country. A great deal of it had been divided up and was under the domination of foreign powers: Spain, France and, above all, Austria, which had taken the lion's share, including Florence, and the whole of Lombardy in the north. It was in Lombardy where Mozart and his father now arrived.

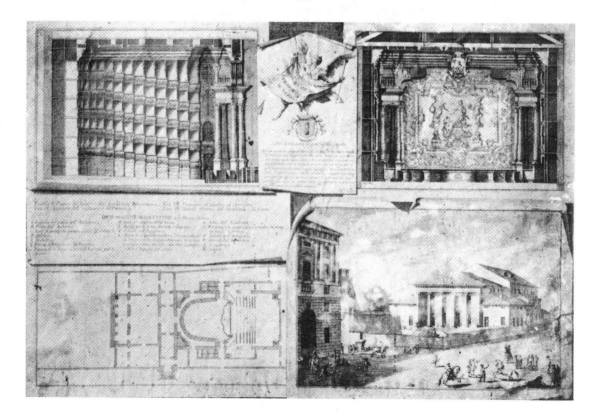

Their first long stop was at Verona, the beautiful medieval city of Romeo and Juliet. They arrived soon after Christmas; Carnival season had started, and Verona was gay and welcoming.

Here for the first time Mozart heard an Italian opera in its native land, and what made the visit even more fun was that the audience, including Mozart, went wearing a mask. Mozart wrote Nannerl a letter in muddled-up German and Italian describing it all (7 January 1770):

Everyone here is *in maschera* just now, and that is very useful, for if you have fastened your mask on your hat, you do not have to take your hat off every time you meet someone you know, and you don't even have to remember their names.

Mozart at the age of fourteen. Portrait by C. B. Cignaroli, Verona, January 1770 (Salzburg Mozarteum)

57

On 5 January Mozart gave his first public concert at the Accademia Filarmonica, and the Italians went wild with excitement and praise. A rich man in the audience insisted on having a portrait done of the boy at once, so Mozart spent the next two days being painted. This picture shows him sitting at the clavier, gorgeously dressed and in a neat wig, with his sense of fun lurking behind his eyes and mouth.

The Italians were so enthusiastic about Mozart's music that when, a few days later, he went to play an organ in a church, he was mobbed in the tumult outside the door. Leopold wrote:

> The throng was so great that we were forced to go through the monastery, where so many people came rushing toward us in a moment that we would not have been able to make our way through if the Fathers, who were already awaiting us at the gate, had not taken us into their midst. When we were done, the tumult was even greater, for everyone wanted to see the little organist. As soon as we were inside the carriage, I ordered the coachman to drive us home, locked the room, and began writing this letter. I had to break away from them all, for otherwise they would not have released us long enough for the writing of a letter.

It took Verona some time to calm down after Mozart's visit.

Next they drove though the bitterly cold winter weather to Mantua. 'Wolfgang looks as if he has been through a campaign, for he is quite coppery, especially about the nose,' wrote his father. His hands were frost-chapped, too, which was painful. After a successful stay in Mantua, they set off again, and arrived in Milan just before Mozart's fourteenth birthday.

They had a very useful friend in Milan—Count Firmian, Governor-General of Lombardy, and a native of Salzburg. Before long he had organised a big public concert (on 23 February); and the Milanese, though interested in this 'marvel of music', went prepared to be critical. Milan demanded the highest standards, being in many ways the musical centre of an intensely musical country.

But, as usual, Mozart confounded his audience with his brilliance. Everyone wanted to meet him, and so Count Firmian organised a *soirée* for the hundred and fifty most important people in Milan. Leopold was very pleased about all this; but Mozart, though he enjoyed it, preferred the Carnival fun in the streets, and the masked balls after the opera. He and Leopold went to the opera as much as they could; Mozart wrote rude comments about them home to Nannerl: '*Prima donna* not so bad, but is rather ancient and ugly as sin. The *seconda donna* looks like a grenadier.'

Giovanni Battista
Martini, know as
Padre Martini
(1706–84). Portrait by
an unknown artist,
c. 1775 (Bologna,
Liceo Musicale)

Then the longed-for thing happened: Mozart was offered a written contract to compose the first opera for the new opera season in Milan, starting the following winter. He left Milan in a blaze of glory, promising to return at the end of the summer in order to start work on the opera.

The Mozarts' next big stop was Bologna, which was almost a place of pilgrimage for all musicians in the eighteenth century. In Bologna lived an old man called Padre Martini, the greatest music scholar and teacher of his time. It was said that he knew everything there was to know about music, and when he praised a composer or a performer their reputations were made for the whole of Europe.

Mozart went to see him and the old man set the boy various

tests, which he passed so easily that Padre Martini was astonished and delighted. So Mozart went on to Florence with the highest of recommendations to back him up.

The ten days in Florence were happy ones, because besides giving several successful concerts Mozart met an old friend from London, Manzuoli.

A letter from Leopold to his wife (3 April) gives us some idea of the Florence visit:

We arrived safely in Florence on the evening of March 30th. On the 31st we spent the whole day indoors and Wolfgang stayed in bed until lunch, as he had caught a slight cold from the rain and the violent wind through which we drove in the mountains. I made him take tea and violet juice and he perspired a little . . . Yesterday evening, April 2nd, we were fetched and driven to the castle outside the town, where we remained until after ten o'clock. Everything went off as usual and the amazement was all the greater as Marchese Ligniville, the Director of Music, who is the finest expert in counterpoint in the whole of Italy, placed the most difficult fugues before Wolfgang and gave him the most difficult themes, which he played off and worked out as easily as one eats a piece of bread. Nardini, that excellent violinist, accompanied him. This afternoon we are going to see Manzuoli, whom we met yesterday in the street and who sends you his greetings. The castrato Nicolini who was with Guadagni in Vienna is here too. I am very sorry that we have to leave on Friday in order to reach Rome in time. I should like you to see Florence itself and the surrounding country and the situation of the town, for you would say that one should live and die here. During these few days I shall see all that there is to be seen. I must close, for the post is leaving. Wolfgang and I send our greetings to all; we kiss you a thousand times and I am your old

Mozart

The Mozarts went on to Rome and arrived in the middle of a very bad thunderstorm. Not daunted in the slightest by the weather, they left their rooms as soon as they had unpacked and went to Michelangelo's Sistine Chapel in the Vatican to hear a performance of a complex choral work, the *Miserere* by Allegri.

When he got home again after the performance, Mozart sat down and wrote the whole piece out from beginning to end accurately from memory. The Romans were amazed when they heard about this, not least because the Papal choir traditionally forbade anyone to make a copy of their music. Concerts were immediately arranged so that they could hear and see this incredible boy.

Mozart enjoyed Rome, though he complained about his cramped quarters in a letter to Nannerl:

60

Duomo, Florence, in the eighteenth century

Rome in the eighteenth century

The Sistine Chapel in the eighteenth century

View of Naples

Oh! I do have a hard time of it—there is only a single bed, and Mama can well guess how much sleep I have with Papa. I am looking forward to moving.

He told her about his sight-seeing:

I have had the honour of kissing St Peter's foot in St Peter's Church, and as I have the misfortune to be on the short side, I, that same old dunce,
>Wolfgang Mozart
>had to be lifted up.

He was always making fun of his own smallness. In another letter to Nannerl from Rome he told her that Manzuoli had been chosen to sing in his opera, which pleased him. The opera was to be called, *Mitridate, Rè di Ponto* (*Mithridatus, King of Pontus*), based on a tragedy by the French writer Racine.

While he was in Rome he composed three symphonies and two arias, and then at the beginning of May he and his father set out for Naples. The journey was supposed to be dangerous because of bandits on the road, but the Mozarts were lucky and did not meet any.

Naples knew all about the boy composer, and gave him a warm welcome. Mozart wrote to Nannerl:

Yesterday we put on new clothes, and looked as handsome as angels. We have seen the King and the Queen of the Two Sicilies at Mass in the Court Chapel. And Vesuvius. Naples is beautiful, but the streets are as crowded as in London or Paris. The beggars are perhaps even worse than those of London in their insolence: the *lazzaroni* as they are called, have their leader, and the King has to bribe him with a regular salary of ten gulden (ten pounds) a month to keep them in order.

. . . Vesuvius is smoking furiously today.

Mozart was in excellent spirits in Naples—he loved the warm southern sun, the success, the trips out on the Mediterranean. He wrote several cheerful letters to Nannerl, full of nonsense, switching gaily from Italian to French, to German and then what he called 'Salzburgish'. To his mother he wrote: 'I too am still alive and always merry as usual and I simply love travelling.'

The whole business of letter-writing in Mozart's time was different from ours. There were no other means of communication and no newspapers to report events in other countries, so all news depended completely on being passed on by letter. Paper was very expensive because it was all hand made, so every inch of a sheet was closely written on. Envelopes had not yet been invented, so the sheets, usually about eight by thirteen inches, were folded twice down the middle, and the address was written on the side which had been left blank on purpose. The letter would then be sealed with wax, and taken by mail-coach slowly to its destination. The way people wrote addresses then seems very vague to us now: for instance, Leopold writing to his wife from Milan just put:

À   Madame Marie Anne Mozart
    Salzburg

(French was used because it was the international language of the educated classes.) But this vague address was quite enough in the eighteenth century: only a small percentage of the population could write anyway, and everybody knew where everyone else in this class lived. One lasting advantage of all these letters, of course, is that they have left us with vivid descriptions of the age and the people. Future biographers will have a less easy time when they come to chronicling our own century.

After a happy, sun-filled month in Naples the Mozarts returned to Rome, driving without stopping for twenty-seven hours, a journey which nowadays can be done in four hours.

As we had only slept for two out of the twenty-seven hours of our journey and had only eaten four cold roast chickens and a piece of bread in the carriage, you can well imagine how hungry, thirsty and sleepy we were,' wrote Leopold to his wife. 'Wolfgang sat down on a chair and at once began to snore and to sleep so soundly that I completely undressed him and put him to bed without his showing the least sign of waking up. . . . When he awoke at nine o'clock in the morning he did not know where he was nor how he had got to bed (27 June).

An extraordinary honour was waiting for Mozart in Rome. On 26 June 1770, Pope Clement IX conferred on Wolfgang Amadeus Mozart the Order of the Golden Spur, in tribute to his musical genius. Two days later the fourteen-year-old Knight of the Golden Spur, wearing the golden cross of the order hanging from a red ribbon around his neck, was given an audience by the Pope himself. Gluck was the only other musician who had ever received this order; and now, as a knight, Mozart had the same social status as the nobility; but unlike Gluck he never made use of the honour; in fact he treated the whole thing almost as a joke. Leopold was far more impressed than was his son; he was at heart rather narrow-minded and conventional.

In July the Mozarts returned to Bologna, where they lived for two months in complete luxury in the beautiful villa of their

Pope Clement with a group of cardinals

PRINCEPS CAETERIQUE

ACADEMICI PHYLHARMONICI.

Omnibus, et singulis praesentes Literas lecturis, felicitatem.

 Uamvis ipsa Virtus sibi, suisque Sectatoribus gloriosum comparet Nomen, attamen pro majori ejusdem majestate publicam in notitiam decuit propagari. Hinc est, quòd hujusce nostrae **PHYLHARMONICAE ACADEMIAE** existimationi, & incremento consulere, singulorumque Academicorum Scientiam, & profectum patefacere intendentes, Testamur *Dnm Wolfgang* ... *Salisburg* ... sub die ... Mensis ... Anni ... inter Academiae nostrae *Magistros Compositores* adscriptum fuisse. Tanti igitur Coacademici virtutem, & merita perenni benevolentiae monumento prosequentes, hasce Patentes, Literas subscriptas, nostrique Confessus Sigillo impresso obsignatas dedimus.
Bononiae ex nostra Residentia die ... Mensis ... Anni ...

Princeps. *Hieronymus Zanti*

a Secretis.

Registr. in Libro Camplono ... pa. ...   Camploncrius.

Certificate of Mozart's reception into the Academy of Bologna

Title page and program of *Mitridate Re di Ponto*

MITRIDATE RE DI PONTO,

DRAMMA PER MUSICA
DA RAPPRESENTARSI
NEL REGIO-DUCAL TEATRO
DI MILANO
Nel Carnovale dell' Anno 1771.
DEDICATO
A SUA ALTEZZA SERENISSIMA
IL
DUCA DI MODENA,
REGGIO, MIRANDOLA ec. ec.
AMMINISTRATORE,
E CAPITANO GENERALE
DELLA LOMBARDIA AUSTRIACA
ec. ec.

IN MILANO, MDCCLXI.
Nella Stamperia di Giovanni Montani
CON LICENZA DE' SUPERIORI

PERSONAGGI.

MITRIDATE, Rè di Ponto, e d'altri Regni, Amante d'Aspasia,
Sig. Cavaliere Guglielmo D'Ettore, Virtuoso di Camera di S. A. S. Elettorale di Baviera.
ASPASIA, promessa sposa di Mitridate, e già dichiarata Regina,
Signora Antonia Bernasconi.
SIFARE, figliuolo di Mitridate, e di Stratonica, amante d'Aspasia,
Sig. Pietro Benedetti, detto Sartorino.
FARNACE, primo figliuolo di Mitridate, amante della medesima,
Sig. Giuseppe Cicognani.
ISMENE, figlia del Re de' Parti, amante di Farnace,
Signora Anna Francesca Varese.
MARZIO, Tribuno Romano, amico di Farnace,
Sig. Gaspare Bassano.
ARBATE, Governatore di Ninfea,
Sig. Pietro Muschietti.

Compositore della Musica.

Il Sig. Cavaliere Amadeo Wolfgango Mozart, Accademico Filarmonico di Bologna, e Maestro della Musica di Camera di S. A. Rma il Principe, ed Arcivescovo di Salisburgo.

ATTO

Mozart wearing the Order of the Golden Spur conferred on him by the Pope in 1770. Anonymous painting, 1777. (Bologna, Liceo Musicale)

patron and friend, Count Pallavicini. They revelled in the countryside around, the hot sun and the cool rooms inside, the fruit unlimited—figs, melons and peaches. Mozart flourished; physically he was growing fast, and Leopold complained that his clothes were becoming too small. His voice broke, too; his singing days were over.

Just before Mozart left Bologna in October he achieved a special distinction at the musical academy which had become so famous under Padre Martini. This Accademia Filarmonica set an examination for membership, which was extremely difficult. Candidates had to be over twenty-one, but a special exception was made for Mozart. He was locked in a room, having been given a complicated type of music to compose. He was finished in an hour; then the judges examined the piece and all of them passed it: Mozart was elected as Honorary member of the Accademia. Many eminent musicians failed to become members, because the test was hard and usually took hours to complete.

By the middle of October, Leopold and his son were back in Milan; the opera had to be finished. Mozart had already written some of it in Bologna—now he had in two months to compose an overture, twenty-two arias, a duet, and a concluding quartet. He had to work so hard and so fast that his fingers ached from writing; Leopold, when it was possible, only allowed him to compose in the long mornings; in the afternoons they went for walks. Otherwise the boy would have cracked under such a strain.

As usual, intrigues and plots against the opera developed; for instance Mozart's enemies incited the *prima donna* to complain that the boy was far too young to compose a real opera. But when Mozart played her arias through for her she was delighted and did not complain again, though less important singers continued to grumble and intrigue, and in the end even Manzuoli did not sing the leading tenor part.

At last, on the day after Christmas came the *première* of Mozart's first big opera *Mitridate, Rè di Ponto*. Mozart himself conducted, from the clavier or cembalo which he was playing in the orchestra. (Conductors in those days did not stand apart, but conducted either from the first violin, or the clavier.) He wore a new suit, of scarlet trimmed with gold braid and lined with sky-blue satin.

The *première* was a sensational triumph; everybody stood up and shouted 'Evviva il maestro!' (Long live the maestro) and wanted encores of every aria. Over twenty performances followed. When Mozart had recovered a little from all the excitement he told Nannerl all about it.

Dearest Sister,

I have not written for a long time, for I was busy with my opera, but as I now have time, I will be more attentive to my duty. The opera, God be praised, is a success, for every evening the theatre is full, much to the astonishment of everyone, for several people say that since they have been in Milan they have never seen such crowds at a first opera. Papa and I, thank God, are well, and I hope that at Easter I shall be able to tell you and Mama everything with my own lips. Addio. I kiss Mama's hand. A propos! Yesterday the copyist called on us and said that he had orders to transcribe my opera for the court at Lisbon. Meanwhile farewell, my dear Mademoiselle sister. I have the honour to be and to remain from now to all eternity

your faithful brother

Altar screen and pulpit
of St. Mark's, Venice.
A photograph
(Anderson)

Because of the enormous success of his opera, Mozart received two more commissions, to write music for the wedding of Maria Theresia's son Ferdinand who was going to be married in Milan in October 1771, and another opera for the Milanese Carnival season. Leopold decided they would go back to Salzburg in between, before Mozart started working on the new commissions.

They returned via Venice which was then celebrating the Carnival season; there were masked balls, parties, operas, and all sorts of fun and horseplay. Mozart, now fifteen, enjoyed it all but Leopold, a bit of a puritan, was slightly shocked, and said he thought Venice was the most dangerous place in all Italy.

They arrived back in Salzburg at the end of March, after fifteen months' absence. Mozart had grown up so much that his mother and sister hardly recognised him. He stayed at home for five months, composing busily, and then in August he and his father went back to Milan for the royal wedding, which was going to happen in October. He started work at once on an operatic ballet, *Ascanio in Alba*; he loved being back in Italy. He described their lodgings to Nannerl:

Above our heads is a violinist, below us another, next door is a singing master who gives lessons, and in the room opposite ours an oboist. This is splendid for composing—it gives you plenty of ideas.

It must sometimes have deafened him as well, but his comment shows what incredible powers of concentration he had.

This time, to Mozart's joy, Manzuoli did sing in his opera: and, as ever, it was a great success. The court gave Mozart a gold watch set with diamonds, as well as his fee, they were so pleased with him. Mozart could write home to his sister that he 'no longer [had] any longing for Salzburg'.

The outcome of all this encouraged Leopold to hope for something more from the Archduke: he wanted his son to get permanent employment as court musician in Milan, and it seemed as if Archduke Ferdinand was in favour of the idea. But Ferdinand's mother Maria Theresia heard about this, and wrote him a crusty letter forbidding him to hire 'a composer or similar useless people', and not to burden himself with people like the Mozarts 'who run about the world like beggars'. So in the end the Archduke refused to employ Mozart, and he and his father returned to Salzburg just before Christmas 1771. They were disappointed, but still hopeful that one day Mozart would find a permanent post in Italy: there was another chance coming up, after all. Mozart still had his commission to

HIERONYMUS IOSEPHUS ex Illma Prosapia
S.R.I. Princ. Colloredo de Waldsee et Mels.
eligitur die 14 Martii 1772.

compose an opera for the Milan season in 1772. They pinned their hopes on that, to keep them cheerful in gloomy, discouraging Salzburg.

In the spring of 1772, when Mozart was sixteen, something happened which was going to affect the rest of his life. The good and kind Archbishop of Salzburg, von Schrattenbach (Mozart used to joke that one pronounced his name by saying 'Sh' and rattling a bag of shot), who had been in Salzburg all Mozart's life, suddenly died. The man who replaced him, Count von Colloredo, came from a great and powerful aristocratic family, and was a stern, proud and haughty man.

He became hated in Salzburg, by the Mozarts as well as everyone else who was not from the same social background as he was.

At first, though, everything went well. Mozart was composing at a very fast rate—in three months he wrote two symphonies, three divertimenti, a duet piano sonata, five songs, an aria, a Mass, litanies and two trio sonatas for the Cathedral. Colloredo rewarded all this work by paying Mozart one hundred and fifty gulden (worth, in present buying power, about £300). He also gave the Mozarts permission to leave again for Milan, because the time was near for Mozart to compose his opera. Father and son went off in October, and the opera called *Lucio Silla* was performed at the end of December. Though the *première* was a success, the Italians did not really like this opera much, because there were new elements in Mozart's musical style which sounded strange to them. There were some fantastic and gloomy scenes of almost Romantic intensity in the opera, and Mozart had composed music to suit their mood. This was not to the Italians' taste, and they never commissioned him to write another opera. Italy was lost to him for good. As Leopold put it 'God probably has something else in mind for us'.

LUCIO SILLA

DRAMMA PER MUSICA

DA RAPPRESENTARSI

NEL REGIO-DUCAL TEATRO
DI MILANO

Nel Carnovale dell' anno 1773.

DEDICATO

ALLE LL. AA. RR.

IL SERENISSIMO ARCIDUCA

FERDINANDO

Principe Reale d' Ungheria , e Boemia , Arciduca d' Austria,
Duca di Borgogna , e di Lorena ec. , Cesareo Reale
Luogo-Tenente , Governatore , e Capitano
Generale nella Lombardia Austriaca ,

E LA

SERENISSIMA ARCIDUCHESSA

MARIA RICCIARDA
BEATRICE D'ESTE

PRINCIPESSA DI MODENA.

IN MILANO,

Preſſo Gio. Batiſta Bianchi Regio Stampatore
Con licenza de' Superiori .

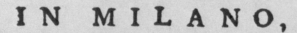

Title page of *Lucio Silla*

Manuscript page from the opera

Archduke Ferdinand of Austria,
to whom Mozart dedicated *Lucio Silla*

Chapter 6

A Love and a Death

'In the ardent regions where all the rest are excited and vehement, Mozart alone is completely self-possessed'—George Bernard Shaw

A new period in Mozart's life, and a less happy one, now started. He was seventeen, and behind him were the easy successes of his childhood and boyhood. He was still the same Wolfgang, gay, nonsensical, untidy and unrealistic, impulsive, scatty and warm-hearted. He was also proud of his genius, and discontented that the great world did not appreciate him properly; it clapped him and then forgot him. And he, like everyone else, needed money in order to eat and go on

An 18th century map
of the archiepiscopate
of Salzburg (Salzburg
Museum)

69

composing. He was poor; he needed a lucrative permanent appointment at a great court—at Vienna, or Munich, or Milan, or Paris. This was the only way in which a musician in the eighteenth century could earn a reasonable living.

Back in Salzburg, Archbishop Colloredo began to show his true colours. He did not like the lively Mozarts: to him they were just two bumptious little men who thought too much of themselves. And he particularly disliked people who were short in stature; so Mozart, who never grew tall, irritated him in every way. The Archbishop had given Mozart a small, ill-paid post as his concert-master, a concert-master being one of the court composers under the *Kapellmeister,* and only grudgingly did he allow him leave of absence that summer to go to Vienna for a brief visit.

In Vienna, Mozart heard the music of Joseph Haydn for the first time. Haydn was already one of the best-known composers in the land, and his music was to make a deep and lasting impression on the young Mozart, whose style soon began to show something of the older man's influence.

During the rest of that year Mozart wrote music in Salzburg at his usual incredible pace. He composed every sort of music, but his favourite was opera: it was his life-long passion, and he was delighted when he was asked to compose a new opera for the Munich Carnival of 1775.

Munich, the
Nymphenburg Castle.
Engraving by
Jungwirth, 1766

Franz Josef Haydn

Maximilian III, Elector of Bavaria

Title page of the German version
of *La Finta Giardiniera*

Manuscript page from the opera

Membership list of the
Salzburg Court
Orchestra, 1775.
Leopold Mozart is
listed as the
Vice-*Kapellmeister*,
Wolfgang as one of the
two *Konzertmeisters*

So in December, Mozart, now nearly nineteen, and his father set out for Munich. It was so cold that the footbags everyone used in coaches were not enough to keep their legs warm, and Leopold ordered an extra large bundle of hay to cover their feet.

The opera was called *La Finta Giardiniera* (*The Disguised Gardener's Girl*) and preparations went well. Even though he had a raging toothache, Mozart was cheerful and full of fun and jokes. The *première* was in the middle of January. In excitement Mozart wrote home:

Thank God! My opera was put on yesterday, the thirteenth, and turned out so well that I cannot possibly describe the storms of applause. In the first place the whole theatre was so jammed full that many people had to be turned away. After every aria there was a regular thunder of clapping and shouts of 'Viva Maestro!' When the opera was over, during the time when the audience is usually quiet until the ballet begins, we heard nothing but clapping and shouts of 'Bravo!'—the applause would die down and start up again, and so on.

Archbishop Colloredo appeared in Munich, missing the opera *première,* obviously uninterested, and heard nothing but praises of Mozart on every side. He shrugged his shoulders and passed it off, but he was increasingly unpleasant to Mozart after that; he quite honestly did not believe Mozart was a genius.

With the success in Munich to give him confidence, Mozart spent the next two years quietly and fairly happily in Salzburg. He wrote among other things a number of divertimenti and occasional pieces, a keyboard concerto, and the five great concertos for violin (written in 1775 for either himself to play or for the leader of the Salzburg orchestra, Antonio Brunetti). Sometimes, however, conditions depressed him, as he showed in a former letter to old Padre Martini in Bologna (4 September 1776):

Reverend Father and Maestro, Most Esteemed Sir,
The respect and esteem I cherish for Your Reverence prompts me to trouble you with this letter and to send you a feeble specimen of my music, submitting it to your sovereign judgment. For last year's Carnival in Munich I composed an *opera buffa, La Finta Giardiniera.* A few days before my departure from that city His Highness the Elector expressed the wish to hear some of my contrapuntal compositions. I was therefore obliged to compose these motets in great haste, in order to have sufficient time for the score to be copied

71

Facsimile of part of
the first movement of
Mozart's Violin
Concerto No. 5 in A
major, December 1775
(Washington, Library
of Congress)

for His Highness and the parts transcribed, so that the motets could be performed in the offertory at High Mass on the following Sunday.

Dearest and most esteemed Father and Master, I earnestly implore you to tell me your opinion of this work candidly and without reserve. We live in this world in order to enlighten one another by interchange of ideas, and to endeavor to further science and the arts. Oh, how often I wish I were closer to you, Reverend Father, in order that I might talk and discuss matters with you. I live in a country where fortune does not favour music, although, aside from those who have left us, we still have excellent teachers and especially composers of great understanding, learning, and taste.

We are ill situated in the theatre for lack of singers. We have no *castrati* and are not likely to have any, for they want to be well paid, and generosity is not one of our faults. I amuse myself meanwhile writing chamber and church music. There are two other contrapuntists here, Michael Haydn and Kajetan Adlgasser. My father is *Kapellmeister* at the cathedral, which provides me with the opportunity to do as much writing for the church as I like. As, moreover, my father has served this court for thirty-six years and knows that the Archbishop does not like to see elderly persons about him, he no longer puts his whole heart into his work and has instead turned to literature, which was always a favourite study of his.

Our church music is quite different from that of Italy, all the more so as a Mass with *Kyrie, Gloria, Credo,* Epistle sonata, Offertory or Motet, *Sanctus,* and *Agnus Dei* must not last longer than three quarters of an hour. This is true even for the most solemn Mass, said by the Prince in person. Special study is requisite for this type of composition, as the Mass must nevertheless have all the instruments, including trumpets, drums, and so on. Alas, how far apart we are, dearest Father and Master. How much I should like to say to you.

Please convey my most respectful greetings to all members of the Accademia Filarmonica. Once again I ask you most sincerely for your favour. It is an unending grief to me that I am so far away from the one person in the world whom I most love, revere, and esteem, and whose

most humble and obedient servant I shall always remain,
Wolfgang Amadeus Mozart

A year later Leopold sent an oil painting of his son to Padre Martini, which shows Mozart as a Knight of the Golden Spur, looking rather solemn (*see* p. 63). He was then twenty-one, and only earning twelve pounds a month from his court post as concert-master.

The situation in Salzburg was now becoming unbearable.

The conference room of the Archbishop's *Residenz* or palace, Salzburg. Many of Mozart's chamber works were written for performance here. A photograph.

Leopold, in a letter to Martini, tells us, for instance, that the Archbishop had openly declared that the young Mozart knew nothing and 'ought to go to a conservatoire in Naples in order to learn music'.

Leopold was so angry that at first he could hardly speak; then a noisy, painful scene followed. Mozart was in an agony of embarrassment: he did not feel the Archbishop was even worth shouting at, and tried to drag his father away.

After this scene he could not wait to leave Salzburg, which he now loathed. The Archbishop dismissed him but retained Leopold, so in September 1777 Mozart left for Munich accompanied this time by his mother. Leopold flatly refused to let him go alone—he knew how impractical and gaily absent-minded his son was. In his heart Mozart was probably relieved not to be with his father: their attitudes had become very different, and Leopold's narrow-mindedness often got on the young man's nerves. He also knew he could twist his warm-hearted but unimaginative mother round his little finger.

Mozart arrived in Munich in the highest spirits. He saw the Elector of Bavaria at his court as soon as was possible; he told him that he had left the court at Salzburg for good. He listed all his past achievements, and asked as humbly as he could for employment. The Elector said there was no vacancy and walked away; Mozart was left bowing. The scene was explicitly described in one of Mozart's letters to his father (29–30 September):

At nine o'clock today, the 30th, I went as arranged with M. Woschitka to Court. Everyone was in hunting dress. Baron Kern was acting chamberlain. I might have gone there yesterday evening, but I did not want to tread on the toes of M. Woschitka, who of his own accord had offered to procure me an audience with the Elector. At ten o'clock he showed me into a little narrow room through which His Highness was to pass on his way to hear Mass before going to hunt. Count Seeau went by and greeted me in the most friendly fashion, saying: 'How do you do, my very dear Mozart!' When the Elector came up to me, I said: 'Your Highness will allow me to throw myself most humbly at your feet and offer you my services'. 'So you have left Salzburg for good?' 'Yes, your Highness, for good.' 'How is that? Have you had a row with him?' 'Not at all, Your Highness. I only asked him for permission to travel, which he refused. So I was compelled to take this step, though indeed I had long been intending to clear out. For Salzburg is no place for me, I can assure you.' 'Good Heavens! There's a young man for you! But your father is still in Salzburg?' 'Yes, your Highness. He too throws himself most humbly at your feet, and so forth. I have been three times to Italy already, I have written three operas, I am a member of the Bologna Academy, where I had to pass a test, at which many maestri have laboured and sweated for four or five hours, but which I finished in an hour. Let that be a proof that I am competent to serve at any Court. My sole wish, however, is to serve your Highness, who himself is such a great——' 'Yes, my dear boy, but I have no vacancy. I am sorry. If only there were a vacancy——' 'I assure your Highness that I should not fail to do credit to Munich.' 'I know. But it is no good, for there is no vacancy here.' This he said as he walked away.

Mozart hated crawling to the nobility, and grew increasingly bad at doing it in spite of Leopold urging him to be more polite. His public concerts in Munich were very successful, but still no one offered him permanent employment; and, most depressing of all, there were no more commissions from Munich to write another opera. Mozart was craving to write an opera: 'I only have to hear talk of an opera, to be in the theatre, to hear the tuning up—and oh, I'm quite beside myself.'

Disgusted with Munich, Mozart and his mother went to Augsburg to stay with cousins. But Augsburg treated Mozart no better: everyone was astounded by his music, but they offered him no permanent post. There was no court at Augsburg, and Mozart used to make fun of the narrow-minded burghers who comprised Augsburg 'society'. The only interesting outcome of the visit, perhaps, was Mozart's encounter with the piano maker, Andreas Stein. In a letter to his father (17 October 1777) he wrote:

Mon trés cher Père!
  This time I shall begin at once with Stein's pianofortes. Before I had seen any of his make, Späth's claviers had always been my favourites. But now I much prefer Stein's, for they damp ever so much better than the Regensburg instruments. When I strike hard, I can keep my finger on the note or raise it, but the sound ceases the moment I have produced it. In whatever way I touch the keys, the tone is always even. It never jars, it is never stronger or weaker or entirely absent; in a word, it is always even. It is true that he does not sell a pianoforte of this kind for less than three hundred gulden, but the trouble and the labour which Stein puts into the making of it cannot be paid for. His instruments have this special advantage over others that they are made with escape action. Only one maker in a hundred bothers about this. But without an escapement it is impossible to avoid jangling and vibration after the note is struck. When you touch the keys, the hammers fall back again the moment after they have struck the strings, whether you hold down the keys or release them. He himself told me that when he has finished making one of these claviers, he sits down to it and tries all kinds of passages,

runs and jumps, and he shaves and works away until it can do anything. For he labours solely in the interest of music and not for his own profit; otherwise he would soon finish his work. He often says: 'If I were not myself such a passionate lover of music and had not myself some slight skill on the clavier, I should certainly long ago have lost patience with my work. But I do like an instrument which never lets the player down and which is durable.' And his claviers certainly do last. He guarantees that the sounding-board will neither break nor split. When he has finished making one for a clavier, he places it in the open air, exposing it to rain, snow, the heat of the sun and all the devils in order that it may crack. Then he inserts wedges and glues them in to make the instrument very strong and firm. He is delighted when it cracks, for he can then be sure that nothing more can happen to it. Indeed he often cuts into it himself and then glues it together again and strengthens it in this way. He has finished making three pianofortes of this kind.

Pianos, however, would not bring Mozart security. He soon left Augsburg for Mannheim.

Mannheim was ruled by another Elector, Karl Theodor, a cultivated and highly intelligent man who encouraged all the arts and had made Mannheim into a unique centre of learning,

Grand piano by Stein, made in the 1770s. (Nürnberg, Germanisch Nationalmuseum)

Charles-Theodore, Elector Palatine (1742-1799)

View of Mannheim

Christian Cannabich, conductor
of the Mannheim orchestra

The Mannheim theater

art, and above all, music. He did this mostly for the greater glory of himself, and to copy the French Court at Versailles, but he appreciated artistic achievement too, and under his rule it flourished.

Mannheim music and the Mannheim orchestra (complete with its renowned wind band and its marvellous clarinets) were famous throughout Europe. They had changed the more rigid seventeenth and early-eighteenth-century style—which is at its best in Johann Sebastian Bach's music, for instance—into something new. They stressed *feeling:* their music appealed to the heart and the emotions as well as the head and the intellect. Their style was Romantic, full of new forms, melodies and harmonies; and above all, they introduced orchestral expression—*crescendo* and *diminuendo.* Before that music was played flatly—the colour and variation did not come from the way one played the notes, loudly or softly, but just from the pattern the notes made. Now in Mannheim the music itself swelled in sound or grew hushed.

One contemporary wrote: 'No orchestra in the world ever surpassed that of Mannheim. Its *forte* is thunder, its *crescendo* a cataract, its *diminuendo* a crystal stream splashing in the distance, its *piano* the breath of spring'.

Mozart's contemporaries were very excited by these new developments and of course they soon carried them to excess. But when Mozart arrived in Mannheim the orchestras there were at their height, and he was impressed and stimulated by the style. He was ripe for new development, and his music soon showed its effect.

Another important thing Mannheim had done for German music was to introduce and encourage opera sung in German rather than Italian. This, too, Mozart made great use of: so far, except for a short piece, he had written all his operas to Italian libretti.

So Mozart came to this exciting and stimulating centre of musicians and composers full of high hopes. He had a successful youth and over three hundred compositions behind him; surely an enlightened city like Mannheim could recognise his genius and help him by giving him a permanent job? Exuberant and happy he plunged into Mannheim life, with his calm mother in the background to organise him and keep his affairs in order.

Every moment of his day was crammed full; with composing, with giving lessons and concerts, with seeing friends and dining out. Mozart wrote to Leopold:

Title page for an early English edition of Mozart's A major Violin Sonata, K.305, written in Mannheim in 1778 (Ateş Orga)

Aloysia Weber (1760–1839). In October 1780 she married the actor and portrait painter Josef Lange (1751–1831), whose unfinished portrait of Mozart is one of the most famous likenesses of the composer

I am writing this at eleven at night because it is the first free time I have had. We cannot very well get up before eight because our rather dark room on the ground floor is not light until half past eight. [They could not afford extra candles.] Then I dress quickly, at ten I sit down to compose until twelve or half after, when I go to the Wendlings [Wendling was first flute in the court orchestra], where I generally continue to compose until half past one. Then we all have dinner.

At three I give lessons to a Dutch officer who pays me, if I'm not mistaken, eighteen gulden [thirty-six pounds] for twelve lessons. At four I get back to our lodgings to teach the daughter of our house [Mozart did this instead of paying rent], but we cannot start until the half hour as we have to wait for candles. At six I go to the Cannabichs [conductor of the Mannheim orchestra] to teach their daughter, and I stay to supper. We talk, and sometimes they play cards; when this happens I take a book out of my pocket and read as I used to do in Salzburg. (20 December 1777)

Mozart hoped to get a job teaching the Elector's children, but after two months' delay, the Elector, not a very musical man, dropped the whole idea. Leopold urged him to leave Mannheim at once, and go on to Paris, the ultimate objective of the tour, but Mozart was enjoying Mannheim too much, and said he would go to Paris in the spring, when travelling conditions would be better for his mother. Anna-Maria had little control over her son; she merely tried to keep his clothes and his finances in order, and was too loving and self-effacing to interfere.

Then, just after his twenty-second birthday, Mozart fell violently in love. The girl's name was Aloysia Weber; she was only fifteen, pretty, with an exquisite voice and was already an accomplished singer. Her father was a poor music copyist, with no prospects of improvement and a large family of daughters to support. Leopold was horrified; he wrote long angry letters about what seemed to him a useless and degrading friendship. Mozart took little notice, and spent all his time with the Webers, writing arias for the enchanting Aloysia and making plans for trips to Italy together, the Webers and he, where he would write an opera and Aloysia would sing in it, conquering Milan with her lovely voice.

Leopold immediately poured cold water on this idea, and ordered Mozart to go to Paris at once. He told him how he was deeply in debt to pay for his son's tour and how he was obliged to dress shabbily and eat cheap food. Mozart's reaction to this was immediate: 'About going to Paris. We shall leave a week today.' He was still under his father's domination, and also deeply touched by the sacrifices Leopold was making for him.

Mozart's mother, Anna-
Maria. Portrait by an
unknown artist,
c. 1775. (Salzburg
Mozarteum)

He and his mother arrived in Paris at the end of March. From the start, Paris was unenthusiastic and depressing. Mozart now hated everything about the French; his heart anyway was in Mannheim, and he wrote long letters to the Webers. Except for the outstanding D major *Paris* symphony (No. 31), he composed little; and he made few visits, because the nobility were cold and insolent, and treated him badly.

Mozart's mother hated Paris as much as he did. She was too simple and natural a person to feel at home in the cold and brittle sophistication of Paris life; she knew nobody, had no spare money to go out and spend, so she stayed inside, unhappy and alone for much of the day, while her son was out composing (they had no clavier in their lodgings). Her health

The Tuileries Palace, where the *Paris* symphony was first performed
in the hall of the Concerts Spirituels

Manuscript from the *Paris* symphony

was already undermined by poverty, rough travelling in draughty coaches, strenuous packing, living in cheap poorly heated rooms, eating bad food and finally drinking Paris water, which was known to be impure. She wrote pathetically to Leopold:

My mode of life is not at all pleasant. I sit alone in the room all day long as if I were under arrest. What is worse, the room is so dark and looks out on such a small courtyard that I cannot see the sun all day long and do not even know what the weather is like. By great effort I can knit a little by the few rays of light that enter. And for this room we have to pay thirty livres a month. The entrance and the stairs are so narrow that it would be impossible to bring up a clavier. Wolfgang must therefore go out to Monsieur Le Gros to compose, because there is a clavier there, and so I do not see him all day and will soon forget completely how to talk.

She fell ill in April, developing a chill and fever, accompanied by diarrhoea and headaches. Mozart became increasingly worried about her, and described the progress of her illness to his father: 'I was very anxious to send for a doctor, but she would not consent; and when I urged her very strongly, she said she had no confidence in a French physician.' At last he managed to find a German doctor, who arrived on 24 June:

On the previous day, when I had wanted him so badly I had a great fright—for all of a sudden she lost her hearing. The doctor (an old German of about seventy) gave her rhubarb powder in wine. I cannot understand that, for people usually say that wine is heating. But when I said so, they all exclaimed: 'How on earth can you say so? Wine is not heating, but strengthening—water is heating'—and meanwhile the poor patient was longing for a drink of fresh water. How gladly would I have given it to her! Most beloved father, you cannot imagine what I endured. . . . I went about as if bereft of my reason.

Anna-Maria became delirious, and on 3 July 1778 she died. Mozart was heartbroken. He did not dare tell his father directly, and got a friend in Salzburg, the Abbé Bullinger, to break the news kindly.

Most beloved Friend!
For you alone.
Mourn with me, my friend! This has been the saddest day of my life—I am writing this at two o'clock in the morning. I have to tell you that my mother, my dear mother, is no more! God has called her to Himself. It was His will to take her, that I saw clearly—so I resigned myself to His will. He gave her to me, so He was able to take her

away from me. Only think of all my anxiety, the fears and sorrows I have had to endure for the last fortnight. She was quite unconscious at the time of her death—her life flickered out like a candle. Three days before her death she made her confession, partook of the Sacrament and received Extreme Unction. During the last three days, however, she was constantly delirious, and today at twenty-one minutes past five o'clock the death agony began and she lost all sensation and consciousness. I pressed her hand and spoke to her—but she did not see me, she did not hear me, and all feeling was gone. She lay thus until she expired five hours later at twenty-one minutes past ten. No one was present but myself, Herr Heina (a kind friend whom my father knows) and the nurse. It is quite impossible for me to describe today the whole course of her illness, but I am firmly convinced that she was bound to die and that God had so ordained it. All I ask of you at present is to act the part of a true friend, by preparing my poor father very gently for this sad news. I have written to him by this post, but only to say that she is seriously ill; and now I shall wait for his answer and be guided by it. May God give him strength and courage! O my friend! Not only am I now comforted, but I have been comforted for some time. By the mercy of God I have borne it all with fortitude and composure. When her illness became dangerous, I prayed to God for two things only—a

Mozart in 1780, detail of family portrait on page 86

Manuscript of the F-minor harpsichord sonata, which Mozart wrote
a few days after his mother died

happy death for her, and strength and courage for myself; and God in His goodness heard my prayer and gave me those two blessings in the richest measure. I beg you, therefore, most beloved friend, watch over my father for me and try to give him courage so that, when he hears the worst, he may not take it too hardly. I commend my sister to you also with all my heart. Go to them both at once, I implore you—but do not tell them yet that she is dead—just prepare them for it. Do what you think best—use every means to comfort them—but so act that my mind may be relieved—and that I may not have to dread another blow. Watch over my dear father and my dear sister for me. Send me a reply at once, I entreat you. Adieu. I remain your most obedient and grateful servant

Wolfgang Amadé Mozart

So Paris had been a tragic fiasco. Mozart promised to go home to Salzburg. He went a long and slow way round, going via Munich, where the Webers now were. They had suddenly become prosperous; Aloysia was earning a large salary as a *prima donna,* and her fame as a singer was spreading. She had come up in the world, and no longer loved the poor struggling composer; she was at heart a cold, calculating girl. Disillusioned and sad, Mozart returned to his hated birthplace, Salzburg.

I swear to you by my honour that I cannot endure Salzburg and all its inhabitants. Their language and their whole way of life are altogether intolerable to me.

Chapter 7

Marriage and Success

'Scarcely any man could stand beside the great Mozart'—Haydn

Mozart's whole tour had been a failure. There were more family debts; to help pay them back Mozart had to become employed again by Archbishop Colloredo, his hated enemy. He was again given the post of concert-master, and paid four hundred and fifty gulden a year.

The tension between father and son increased during the next year in Salzburg. Mozart was now nearly twenty-four, and yet Leopold continued to control his life, encouraging his music, but criticising every other thing about him. Leopold never made any allowances for Mozart's untidiness, pride, moodiness and extravagance with money; he knew his son was a genius, but expected him to behave as if he were an ordinary person, and a rather dull and money-minded one at that. Poor Mozart could never forget about money all his life. He was often penniless, underpaid for all he did, and always in search of a lucrative, permanent post which would free him once and for all from financial worry. Noblemen who were impressed by his genius nearly always gave him a useless present instead of the solid cash which he needed. After a typical visit to a court official who had asked him to come and collect his reward, he wrote to his father:

No money, but a fine gold watch. At the moment ten carolins would have suited me better than the watch, which, including the chains and the mottoes, has been valued at twenty. What one needs on a journey is money; and, let me tell you, I now have five watches. I am therefore seriously thinking of having an additional watch pocket on each leg of my trousers so that when I visit some great lord I shall wear both watches . . . so that it will not occur to him to present me with another one.

A concert in Salzburg
Cathedral. An
engraving

But when Mozart did have short bursts of affluence, he had
no idea how to save money for a needy period. Leopold, on the
other hand, was well aware of the value of money, and longed
to be rich, both for the comfort and the worldly position wealth
would bring. Mozart only wanted enough money to make him

free, free from the need to flatter and beg favours of the nobility, free from having to grind away giving lessons to fat, dull, unmusical women, free to compose all he wanted, particularly his beloved operas.

In Salzburg he felt imprisoned. 'When I play, or when some of my pieces are performed, it's as though the audience was made of nothing but tables and chairs,' he complained. 'You are sometimes too proud,' said Leopold. Mozart, disinclined to argue, went on his own way. Strangely enough none of the works he wrote during this depressing year showed any signs of the tensions and stresses he was living through.

In view of life in Salzburg he was, not surprisingly, overjoyed when Munich asked him to write an opera for the Carnival of 1781. In November 1780 the Archbishop gave him six weeks' leave of absence, and off went Mozart to write *Idomeneo*. There were the usual rows and intrigues in Munich, and the rush to finish in time, but when *Idomeneo* was finally given at the end of January it was an instant, resounding success. Mozart stayed on to enjoy Munich; everyone fêted him.

The Mozart family. From a painting by Johann Nepomuk de la Croce, 1780–81. The mother's portrait hangs on the wall (Salzburg Mozarteum)

IDOMENEO.

DRAMMA

PER

MUSICA

DA RAPPRESENTARSI

NEL TEATRO NUOVO DI

CORTE

PER COMANDO

DI S. A. S E.

CARLO TEODORO

Conte Palatino del Rheno, Duca dell'
alta, e bafsa Baviera, e del Palatinato
Superiore, etc. etc. Archidapifero,
et Elettore, etc. etc.

NEL CARNOVALE

1781.

La Poesia è del Signor Abate Giambattista Varesco
Capellano di Corte di S. A. R. l'Arcivescovo, e Principe di Salisburgo.
La Musica è del Signor Maestro Wolfgango Amadeo Mozart Academico di Bologna, e di Verona, in
in attual servizio di S. A. R. l'Arcivescovo, e Principe
di Salisburgo.
La Traduzione è del Signor Andrea Schachtner,
pure in attual servizio di S. A. R. l'Arcivescovo, e
Principe di Salisburgo.

MONACO,

Appresso Francesco Giuseppe Thuille.

Title page of *Idomeneo*

Model of stage set from the original Munich production of *Idomeneo*

The six-week leave of absence became four months, and eventually the Archbishop, now at the end of his patience, and in Vienna for the spring, ordered Mozart to join him there at once. Vienna—that promised well.

He had an unpleasant shock in store: he was treated by the Archbishop as an unimportant servant, and made to eat and share quarters with the valets. After three weeks, when the Archbishop rudely ordered his musicians back to Salzburg just as Mozart was receiving new commissions, matters came to a head. Twice he had controlled himself and avoided a row, but this time Colloredo had gone too far. Mozart did not leave Vienna when he was supposed to, and Colloredo called him into his private apartments.

Mozart described what happened in a letter written to Leopold on 9 May 1781:

I am still seething with rage! And you, my dearest and most beloved father, are doubtless in the same condition. My patience has been so long tried that at last it has given out. I am no longer so unfortunate as to be in Salzburg service. Today is a happy day for me. Just listen.

Twice already that—I don't know what to call him—has said to my face the greatest *sottises* and *impertinences,* which I have not repeated to you, as I wished to spare your feelings, and for which I only refrained from taking my revenge on the spot because you, my most beloved father, were ever before my eyes. He called me a <rascal> and a <dissolute fellow> and told me to be off. And I—endured it all, although I felt that not only my honour but yours also was being attacked. But, as you would have it so, I was silent. Now listen to this. A week ago the footman came up unexpectedly and told me to clear out that very instant. All the others had been informed of the day of their departure, but not I. Well, I shoved everything into my trunk in haste, and old Madame Weber has been good enough to take me into her house, where I have a pretty room. Moreover, I am living with people who are obliging and who supply me with all the things which one often requires in a hurry and which one cannot have when one is living alone. I decided to travel home by the ordinaire on Wednesday, that is, today, May 9th. But as I could not collect the money still due to me within that time, I postponed my departure until Saturday. When I presented myself today, the valets informed me that the Archbishop wanted to give me a parcel to take charge of. I asked whether it was urgent. They told me, 'Yes, it is of the greatest importance.' 'Well,' said I, 'I am sorry that I cannot have the privilege of serving His Grace, for (on account of the reason mentioned above) I cannot leave before Saturday. I have left this house, and must live at my own expense. So it is evident that I cannot leave Vienna until I am in a position to do so. For surely no one will ask me to ruin myself.' Kleinmayr, Moll, Bönike and the two valets, all said that I was perfectly right. When I went in to the

Archbishop . . . his first words were:—*Archbishop:* 'Well, young fellow, when are you going off?' *I:* 'I intended to go tonight, but all the seats were already engaged.' Then he rushed full steam ahead, without pausing for breath—I was the <most dissolute fellow he knew—no one> served him so badly as I did—I had better leave today or else he would write home and have my <salary> stopped. I couldn't get a word in edgeways, for he blazed away like a fire. I listened to it all very calmly. He lied to my face that my salary was five hundred gulden, called me <a scoundrel, a rascal, a vagabond>. Oh, I really cannot tell you all he said. At last my blood began to boil, I could no longer contain myself and I said, 'So Your Grace is not satisfied with me?' 'What, you dare to threaten me—you <scoundrel?> There is the <door>! Look out, for I will have nothing more to do with such <a miserable wretch>'. At last I said: 'Nor I with you!' 'Well, be off!' When leaving the room, I said, 'This is final. You shall have it tomorrow in writing.' Tell me now, most beloved father, did I not say the word too late rather than too soon? Just listen for a moment. My honour is more precious to me than anything else and I know that it is so to you also. Do not be the least bit anxious about me. I am so sure of my success in Vienna that I would have resigned even without the slightest reason; and now that I have a very good reason—and that too thrice over—I cannot make a virtue of it. Au contraire, I had twice played the coward and I could not do so a third time.

Vienna, St. Peter's Church and Square. Mozart lived in the house on the right after leaving Salzburg in 1781. An engraving

Constanze Weber
(1763–1842) at about
the time of her
marriage to Mozart,
1782

For all Mozart's pleas, Leopold's 'honour', however, was different from his son's, and he did his best to stop the resignation. But Mozart was determined, and there followed two further noisy rows in which Colloredo's agent tried to persuade him to return to Salzburg, and refused to accept his resignation. The Archbishop had to admit to himself that he found Mozart useful and, with his rapidly increasing fame, an asset in the eyes of the musical world. But in the end Mozart was so rude that Colloredo had him propelled out of the palace literally with a kick on his behind. The date was 8 June 1781. Their connection was finally severed and Mozart was free. 'The heart ennobles a man,' he wrote to his father. 'And although I am no count I may well have more honour in me than many a count. And lackey or count, whoever insults me is a rogue.'

Mozart now moved in as a lodger with the Webers, who were back in his life and living in Vienna. Weber had died, leaving his wife and four daughters penniless. Aloysia had married at once, and she and her husband paid a substantial sum regularly to Madame Weber, who earned the rest of her income by letting rooms to lodgers. She was a heartless, scheming woman—Mozart himself later described her as 'a false, malicious person'—and was determined to trap him into marriage with one of her daughters, even though the one he first loved was now unobtainable.

So Madame Weber, Josepha, Constanze and Sophie looked after Mozart's every need, spoilt him and cosseted him. He loved it. He got up early, composed all morning, dressed when he felt like it, had all his meals when it suited him—sometimes if he were composing in the evenings, supper would be postponed until ten o'clock. He was happy, hard-working and carefree.

Leopold, on the other hand, was cross and worried. He did not trust the Webers, and was sure their easy-going Bohemian way of life had a bad effect on Mozart. He was also sure that one of the girls was going to trap Mozart into marriage, and rumours from Vienna that Mozart was in love with Constanze made him write some angry letters. These rumours forced Mozart to change his lodgings, to his own annoyance, but he wrote cheerfully to reassure his father: 'If ever there was a time when I thought less of getting married, it is most certainly now!'

He said that he had not fallen in love with Constanze; but in fact he had. She was eighteen, not pretty, but courageous and understanding. Mozart enjoyed her company, and was always going to see her.

So far Vienna was opening all doors to Mozart. He had

several regular lessons to give, which at six ducats a time paid him well. He published six violin sonatas, and they were an instant success. The announcement of their issue (8 December) read: 'Obtainable at Artaria and Co., art dealers in the Kohlmarkt, opposite the Michaelskirche, are six newly published sonatas for clavier with accompanying violin, Op. 2, of the well known and widely acclaimed composer Wolfgang Amadé Mozart (five gulden)'. In Köchel's definitive catalogue of Mozart's works, first published in Leipzig in 1862, the six sonatas are listed respectively under Köchel (or K.) numbers 296 and 376–80.

He also gave well-attended concerts, and on 24 December took part, at the Emperor's invitation, in a celebrated contest with Muzio Clementi. Mozart described the occasion:

Muzio Clementi (1746–1832), composer, pianist and music publisher. He settled in London in 1798. Engraving by J. Niedl after Thomas Hardy

After we had exchanged compliments by the dozen, the Emperor proposed that Clementi play first. '*La santa chiesa cattolica*,' he said, because Clementi is a Roman. He preluded and played a sonata. Then the Emperor said to me: '*Allons*, fire away.' I also preluded and played variations. Then the Duchess handed over some sonatas by Paisiello, wretchedly written in his own hand. I had to play the allegros and he the andantes and rondos of these. Then we picked a theme from them and developed it on two pianofortes. One odd thing was that I had borrowed Countess Thun's pianoforte, but used it only when I played alone, because that was the Emperor's wish. And mark this, the other instrument was out of tune, and three of the keys stuck. 'It doesn't matter,' the Emperor said. I choose to put the best construction on that, namely that the Emperor already knows my skill and knowledge of music and merely wanted to show me off properly to the foreigner. Incidentally, I have heard from a very

Blonde's aria 'Welche Wonne, welche Lust' from *Il Seraglio*. Autograph facsimile (Tübingen, Universitätsbibliothek)

reliable source that he was thoroughly satisfied with me. He was very gracious and talked to me a great deal in private. He also spoke with me about my marriage. Who knows—perhaps—what do you think? It is always worth trying.

Clementi had this to say of Mozart's playing:

I had never before heard anyone play with such intelligence and grace. I was particularly overwhelmed by an adagio and by several of his extempore variations for which the Emperor chose the theme, and which we were required to vary alternately, accompanying one another.

Another important event of the year was that in the July he was asked to write an opera. It was to be called *The Abduction from the Seraglio*—a story about a beautiful Spanish girl who was imprisoned by a Turkish Pasha in his harem (Seraglio) and who was eventually rescued by her lover. The opera was to be sung in German, which was an innovation; up till now, opera libretti had been in Italian. In writing the *Seraglio* (*Die Entführung aus dem Serail*) Mozart created the first real

An Ottoman Janissary band of the kind that inspired 'Turkish music' and 'Turkish' themes throughout the 18th and early 19th centuries. The sound of these instruments influenced not only Mozart but also Gluck and Haydn, as well as Beethoven in his Ninth Symphony. A plate from *Les anciens costumes de l'Empire Ottoman* by Arif Pasa (Paris 1864)

'character' in opera—up till now operatic parts had just been something in which good singers could show off their singing, and were not expected to behave like live human beings. But in the *Seraglio* Mozart created a Turkish servant called Osmin, who comes completely alive: he is a huge, greedy, bad-tempered old man, who is fooled in the end, to everyone's joy and delight. After this start, Mozart's later operas are full of splendid characters, both good and bad, comic and tragic.

But the *Seraglio* was not performed until a year later, and in between, Mozart's life was changed completely; he became engaged to Constanze Weber. During all that year he had been falling more deeply in love with her, almost without him realising it. Madame Weber saw this happening, and plotted to force Mozart's hand by spreading vicious gossip about Vienna; these rumours said he had dishonoured Constanze and was not serious in his intentions towards her. Madame Weber then demanded that Mozart should marry Constanze at once before her reputation was quite ruined; otherwise they must part for ever. Mozart was now almost twenty-six, and knew his own mind; he asked Constanze to marry him. He wrote to his father on 15 December 1781:

You demand an explanation of the words in the closing sentence of my last letter! Oh, how gladly would I have opened my heart to you long ago, but I was deterred by the reproaches you might have made to me for *thinking of such a thing at an unseasonable time*—although indeed thinking can never be unseasonable. Meanwhile I am very anxious to secure here a small but *certain* income, which, together with what chance may provide, will enable me to live here quite comfortably—and then—to marry! You are horrified at the idea? But I entreat you, dearest, most beloved father, to listen to me. I have been obliged to reveal my intentions to you. You must, therefore, allow me to disclose to you my reasons, which, moreover, are very well founded. The voice of nature speaks as loud in me as in others, louder, perhaps, than in many a big strong lout of a fellow. I simply cannot live as most young men do in these days. In the first place, I have too much religion; in the second place, I have too great a love of my neighbour and too high a feeling of honour to seduce an innocent girl; and, in the third place, I have too much horror and disgust, too much dread and fear of diseases and too much care for my health to fool about with whores. So I can swear that I have never had relations of that sort with any woman. Besides, if such a thing had occurred, I should not have concealed it from you; for, after all, to err is natural enough in a man, and to err *once* would be mere weakness—although indeed I should not undertake to promise that if I had erred once in this way, I should stop short at one slip. However, I stake my life on the truth of what I have told you. I am well aware that this reason (powerful as it is) is not urgent enough. But owing to my disposition,

93

which is more inclined to a peaceful and domesticated existence than to revelry, I who from my youth up have never been accustomed to look after my own belongings, linen, clothes and so forth, cannot think of anything more necessary to me than a wife. I assure you that I am often obliged to spend unnecessarily, simply because I do not pay attention to things. I am absolutely convinced that I should manage better with a wife (on the same income which I have now) than I do by myself. And how many useless expenses would be avoided! True, other expenses would have to be met, but—one knows what they are and can be prepared for them—in short, one leads a well-ordered existence. A bachelor, in my opinion, is only half alive. Such are my views and I cannot help it. I have thought the matter over and reflected sufficiently, and I shall not change my mind. But who is the object of my love? Do not be horrified again, I entreat you. Surely not one of the Webers? Yes, one of the Webers—but not Josefa, nor Sophie, but Constanze, the middle one . . . She is not ugly, but at the same time far from beautiful. Her whole beauty consists in two little black eyes and a pretty figure. She has no wit, but she has enough common sense to enable her to fulfil her duties as a wife and mother. It is a downright lie that she is inclined to be extravagant. On the contrary, she is accustomed to be shabbily dressed, for the little that her mother has been able to do for her children, she has done for the two others, but never for Constanze. True, she would like to be neatly and cleanly dressed, but not smartly, and most things that a woman needs she is able to make for herself; and she dresses her own hair every day. Moreover she understands housekeeping and has the kindest heart in the world. I love her and she loves me with all her heart. Tell me whether I could wish myself a better wife?

Constanze Weber. A portrait by Josef Lange, 1782 (University of Glasgow)

Leopold still felt, quite rightly, that Mozart was being blackmailed, and wrote opposing the whole idea of marriage, withholding his consent to it. Mozart wrote back in desperation:

You cannot oppose it—and surely you don't! Your letters make that clear to me. For she's a fine honest girl of good parentage. I am able to support her. We love one another and need one another.

Leopold still had not given his consent by 4 August 1782, and on that day Mozart and Constanze Weber were married in St. Stephen's Cathedral. Three days later Mozart wrote to his father with an account of the wedding:

Well, it is over! I only ask your forgiveness for my too hasty trust in your fatherly love. In this frank confession you have a fresh proof of my love of truth and hatred of a lie. Next post-day my dear wife will ask her dearest, most beloved Papa-in-law for his fatherly blessing and her beloved sister-in-law for the continuance of her most valued

Address of a letter from Mozart to Constanze before they were married

Constanze, aged 17

Marriage contract of Mozart and Constanze

Constanze in 1783

Mozart in 1783

Der Stock am Eisen Platz.   La Place du Stock am Eisen.

Vienna, the Stock in Eisen Square and St. Stephen's Cathedral. Coloured engraving by Karl Schütz, 1779

friendship. No one was present at the wedding save her mother and her youngest sister, Herr von Thorwart as guardian and witness for both of us, Herr von Cetto, district councillor, who gave away the bride, and Gilowsky as my best man. When we had been joined together, both my wife and I began to weep. All present, even the priest, were deeply touched and all wept to see how much our hearts were moved. Our whole wedding feast consisted of a supper given for us by the Baroness von Waldstädten, which indeed was more princely than baronial.

Mozart and his bride at once set up house on their own: Madame Weber's offer that they should live with her was firmly refused. Mozart had no illusions about his mother-in-law, although he did not seem to have realised the full extent of her trickery.

At last Mozart was free of his father's authority: he had asserted his own will and shown that from then on he would decide for himself both on personal and business matters, whatever the outcome. Fond though he was of the old man, Leopold and he saw eye to eye on one subject only—music.

95

And even in that Leopold felt his son was not completely fulfilling the genius he had shown as a child and boy. Mozart, on the other hand, felt happy and confident. Just before his marriage the *Seraglio* had been performed and became overnight a first-class success—everybody was talking about it. Even the great poet Goethe said that the opera 'put everything else in the shade'. The triumphant young composer could write that 'people are simply crazy about this opera'. By now Mozart was sure that some permanent job at the Emperor's court would be offered him soon: all Vienna knew him, and he had high hopes for his future in that city of music.

Mozart at the Piano. Detail from an unfinished oil on canvas by Mozart's brother-in-law, Josef Lange, *c.* 1782–83

Chapter 8

Vienna and the Mozarts

'In order to win applause one must write stuff which is so inane that a cabby could sing it, or so unintelligible that it pleases precisely because no sensible man can understand it'—Mozart to his father

The world in which Mozart spent the final ten years of his life was one of upheaval and change. The last twenty years of the eighteenth century brought about changes in living, thinking and governing which are still with us now. In those twenty years the feudal system in Europe—of lord over serf—was finally shattered by the French Revolution of 1789. Millions of peasants were in revolt against a social system which they hated because it was built on ancient rights and privileges based on the blood that flowed in a man's veins rather than the merits he possessed. If you were born a peasant, a peasant you probably died. We have seen Mozart himself rebelling against this system; he, like his contemporaries, felt that a man's honour lay in his heart, his brains and his abilities, and not just in his blue blood if he happened to be born with it, and his aristocratic position.

All over Europe this change in ideas was taking place; and it boiled over first in France. The Revolution went too far the other way, and there was unnecessary and horrible bloodshed; the principles of Liberty, Equality, Fraternity were almost drowned under all the crimes.

Of course, as with all big historical changes, those nearest to it in time saw it much less clearly than we do looking back. Habsburg Vienna in the 1780s and the 1790s was still the same gay sophisticated city, with life revolving, as it always had, around the Emperor's court.

Joseph II, Maria Theresia's son, was now Emperor. He was a good man, though not a good ruler; and unlike his mother he encouraged the arts, particularly music. He loved Italian music,

98

Antonio Salieri
(1750–1825), friend of
Haydn and Beethoven,
enemy of Mozart

and housed an entire Italian opera company in his palace permanently. There were Italian composers and musicians by the dozen in Vienna and when Mozart came along and started to take the city by storm they were furiously jealous. They spread outrageous lies and unpleasant stories about him, and would quite cheerfully have cut his throat or poisoned him if they had had a chance. This bitter feud went on all Mozart's life, led by a court musician called Salieri who hated him.

The Mozarts' married life had begun stormily in 1782, and it never became a calm peaceful relationship. Mozart adored Constanze in spite of her slackness about personal and household affairs, her unreliability and her selfishness; but with these qualities she did not create the happy home life he needed so much. However Constanze was not a bad woman, and being married to a lively, changeable genius must have been very difficult; she may have been the wrong wife for Mozart, but he was also the wrong husband for her. She needed

99

Below
Cadenza to the
first movement
of Mozart's Piano
Concerto in A major,
K.414 (1782-83).
Autograph facsimile
(Tübingen,
Universitätsbibliothek)

a solid respectable man of ordinary abilities to keep her under control. (After Mozart's death she remarried and her second husband was just such a man as this. Constanze then became a good wife and mother.)

In the year of his marriage Mozart started a period which was excitingly successful. He did not mind the fact he had not yet been offered a permanent post at court—he was doing so well as a free-lance. Even the Italians' efforts to ruin the *première* of *Il Seraglio* by hissing and booing all the way through the first act had no effect. He had enough pupils to be able to live well off the proceeds of giving lessons; though it did mean that his precious mornings, during which he loved to compose, were all used up with teaching. He often got up at six in the morning in his first years in Vienna, so that he could fit in everything. He would teach till about two, then dine, and then if there were no concerts to give, spend the late afternoon and evening composing.

But as he grew more popular he found he was always in demand, and his spare time was almost non-existent. He was very sociable and loved balls and parties; the first winter after

Opposite page
An allemande danced
at a *bal paré*. Engraving
after Augustin de St.
Aubin, 1773. In his
Reminiscences (1826)
Michael Kelly wrote
that 'Vienna then
[1776] was a place
where pleasure was the
order of the day and
night . . . The people
of Vienna were in my
time dancing mad; as
the Carnival
approached, gaiety
began to display itself
on all sides and when
it really came, nothing
could exceed its
brilliance. The ridotto
rooms, where the
masquerades took place
were in the [Imperial]

100

palace, and spacious and commodious as they were, they were actually crammed with masqueraders. I never saw, or indeed heard of any suite of rooms, where elegance and convenience were more considered; for the propensity of the Vienna ladies for dancing and going to Carnival masquerades was so determined, that nothing was permitted to interfere with their enjoyment of their favourite amusement—nay, so notorious was it that for the sake of ladies in the family way, who could not be persuaded to stay at home, there were apartments prepared, with every convenience for their accouchement, should they be unfortunately required. And I have been gravely told and almost believe it that there have actually been instances of utility of the arrangement. The ladies of Vienna are particularly celebrated for their grace and movements in waltzing of which they never tire. For my own part I thought waltzing from ten at night until seven in the morning, a continual whirligig; most tiresome to the eye and ear—to say nothing of any worse consequences'

their marriage he and Constanze gave one which began at six in the evening and ended at seven in the morning.

When there were concerts to be given they were an invariable success. One on 11 March 1783 was recalled by Mozart:

The theatre was very full, and I was again so warmly received by the public that I cannot help being truly pleased. I had already left the stage, but the clapping would not stop, and I had to repeat the rondo. It was a veritable downpour. . . . Gluck had the box next to the Langes, in which my wife was also seated. He could not praise the symphony and aria enough, and invited all four of us to dine with him next Sunday.

Another followed less than a fortnight later, on 23 March:

The theatre could not possibly have been fuller, and all the boxes were occupied. But what pleased me most was that His Majesty the Emperor was present. And how delighted he was, and how loudly he applauded me. It is his custom to send the money to the box office before he enters the theatre; otherwise I could justly have expected much more, for his pleasure was boundless. He sent twenty-five ducats.

In June 1783 his first son was born. When Constanze was ready to travel again they decided to go to Salzburg—it would be her first meeting with her father-in-law. They left their son with foster-parents; this was a common habit in the eighteenth century, for very few women fed their own babies, except those who were peasants, and the food given to babies was often

101

quite unsuitable for them. The visit to Leopold went well; the old man had become reconciled to Constanze, who was very charming when she wished to be so. But when they got back to Vienna three months later they discovered the little boy had died. They were upset, but people were used to babies dying: because of wrong feeding and lack of hygiene the infant death-rate was ten times higher then than now. Mozart was to have six children, but only two of them lived.

Winter came again and, if anything, Mozart's life was even fuller and busier. Early in the new year, 1784, he decided to start making a list of his works—his papers were in their usual mess, and this seemed one way of organising things better. He had already written 450 works, which he knew it would be hopeless to try to remember in detail; so he started at that point and kept the list up till he died. In all, during the whole of his life, he wrote over 620 compositions.

He gave concerts in the evenings throughout that winter. He had to compose new pieces for these, and as he had so little time, they were often written right up to the last minute. Sometimes when he was accompanying someone else, he

The beginning of the third movement of the Horn Concerto in E flat, K.417, written in 1783 for the celebrated horn player Ignaz Leutgeb. The manuscript, formerly in the Preussische Staatsbibliothek, Berlin, was lost in 1945

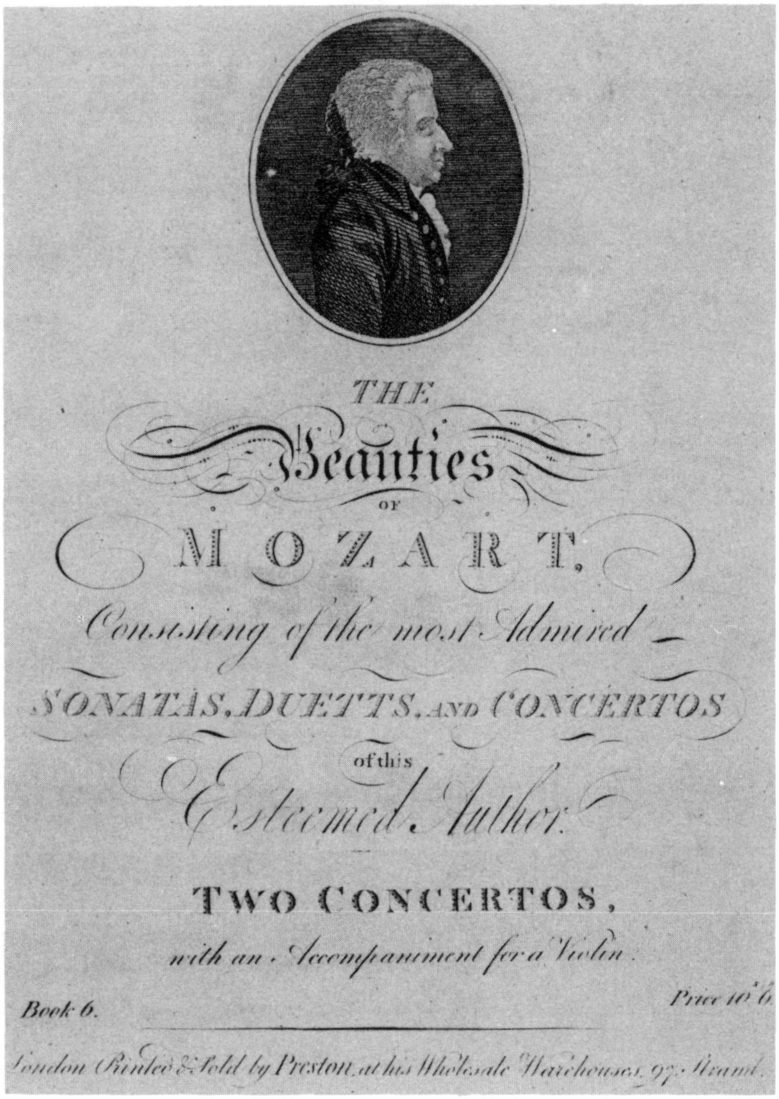

Title page for an early
English edition of
Mozart's Piano
Concerto in F major,
K.459, written in Vienna
in 1784 (Ateş Orga)

THE
Beauties
OF
MOZART,
Consisting of the most Admired
SONATAS, DUETTS, AND CONCERTOS
of this
Esteemed Author

TWO CONCERTOS,
with an Accompaniment for a Violin.

Book 6.   Price 10.6.

London Printed & Sold by Preston at his Wholesale Warehouse, 97 Strand.

improvised his own part at the performance.

It was to be expected that after this pressure of work, Mozart
would fall very ill in the spring. Every year of his life he
suffered from some illness or other, and was usually in bed for
anything up to three weeks. This was not really surprising,
because since he was six he had been living a full, hectic life in
which there was rarely a quiet spell. He caught cold easily, and
grew feverish; and doctors' prescriptions in the eighteenth
century were often so wrong that it was a wonder their
treatment alone did not kill him off, as it did so many people
then. But Mozart's recoveries from ill health were as
miraculous as the ceaseless outpouring of his music.

Joseph Haydn
(1732–1809). Portrait
in oils by Thomas
Hardy, 1791 (London,
Royal College of
Music)

This time he was very seriously ill with what seems now like
acute kidney trouble. It took him the whole summer to get
better, but soon after his recovery Constanze had a second
baby—a little boy, who lived. He was called Karl.

Leopold, who was a lonely old man now, living on his own,
decided to come to Vienna for a visit. Nannerl had just got
married, to the whole family's joy. She was over thirty, and
Leopold had been sure she was 'on the shelf'. He was delighted
when she married, but it left him quite alone.

He arrived in Vienna in January 1785, and was rushed by his
famous son into the whirl of the Viennese musical world. On
his first evening he was taken to a concert Mozart was giving,
and was most impressed by the high standard of the orchestra,
the singers, and, being Leopold, by the amount of nobility in

Mozart and Haydn

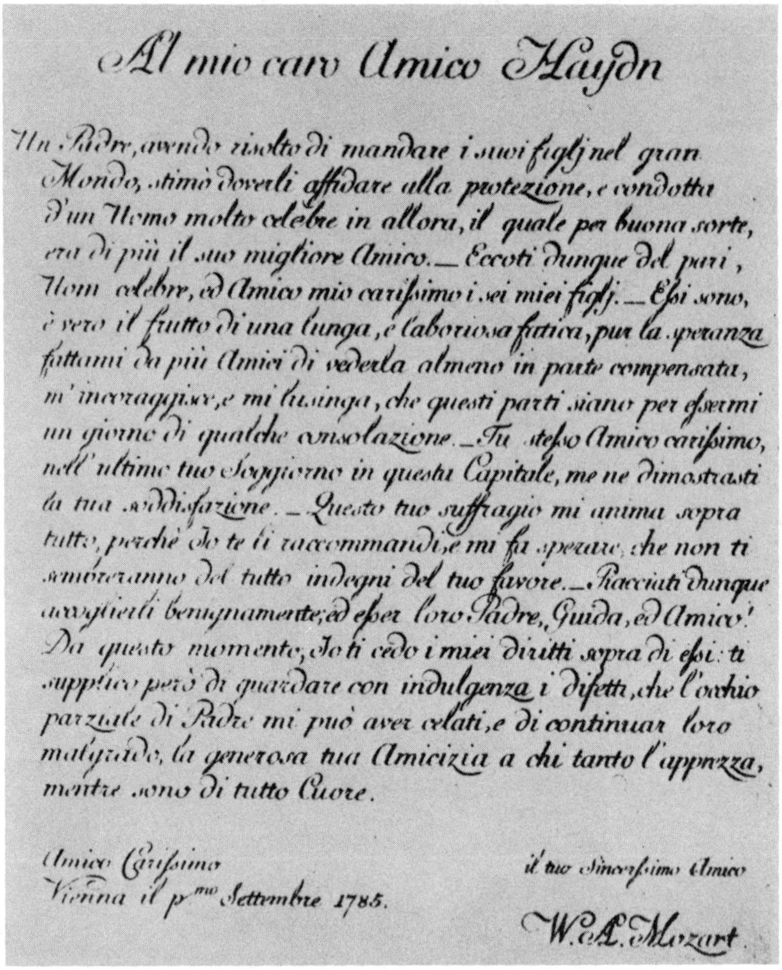

Dedication page of the Haydn quartets

Al mio caro Amico Haydn

Un Padre, avendo risolto di mandare i suoi figlj nel gran
Mondo, stimò doverli affidare alla protezione, e condotta
d'un Uomo molto celebre in allora, il quale per buona sorte,
era di più il suo migliore Amico. — Eccoti dunque del pari,
Uom celebre, ed Amico mio carissimo i sei miei figlj. — Essi sono,
è vero il frutto di una lunga, e laboriosa fatica, pur la speranza
fattami da più Amici di vederla almeno in parte compensata,
m'incoraggisce, e mi lusinga, che questi parti siano per essermi
un giorno di qualche consolazione. — Tu stesso Amico carissimo,
nell'ultimo tuo Soggiorno in questa Capitale, me ne dimostrasti
la tua soddisfazione. — Questo tuo suffragio mi anima sopra
tutto, perchè Io te li raccommandi, e mi fa sperare, che non ti
sembreranno del tutto indegni del tuo favore. — Piacciati dunque
accoglierli benignamente, ed esser loro Padre, Guida, ed Amico!
Da questo momento, Io ti cedo i miei diritti sopra di essi: ti
supplico però di guardare con indulgenza i difetti, che l'occhio
parziale di Padre mi può aver celati, e di continuar loro
malgrado, la generosa tua Amicizia a chi tanto l'apprezza,
mentre sono di tutto Cuore.

Amico Carissimo   il tuo Sincerissimo Amico
Vienna il p.mo Settembre 1785.

                                               W. A. Mozart.

DAS

LOB DER FREUNDSCHAFT

KANTATE

von

W. A. Mozart.

Partitur.

Bei Breitkopf und Härtel in Leipzig
Pr. 1 Thlr.

Title page of the Masonic Cantata

the audience. The next night Mozart introduced his father to Joseph Haydn; he had come for a musical evening at the Mozarts' house, and at the end of it he said to Leopold:

I, as an honest man, tell you before God that your son is the greatest composer I know in person or by name. He has taste and, moreover, the most thorough knowledge of composition.

Leopold realised at last that all his sacrifices, worries and spiritual anxieties over his son had not been in vain: Mozart had fulfilled his genius; a man who was great himself proclaimed him greater. Mozart that autumn returned Haydn's compliment in the form of a dedication in Artaria's first edition of the six string quartets, K. 387, 421, 428, 458, 464 and 465. The inscription was elaborate:

A father about to send his sons into the great world naturally desires to confide them to the protection and guidance of a celebrated man, who happily has also been his best friend. Most celebrated man and my dearest friend, take these six children of mine. They are, in truth, the fruit of long and laborious toil, but the hope some friends have given me that this toil may be at least partly rewarded encourages me, and I flatter myself that these creations of mine may someday provide me with consolation. You yourself, my dearest friend, expressed your pleasure in these compositions during your last stay in this capital. Your approval is the chief thing that inspires me to place my children in your arms, and leads me to hope that they may not be altogether unworthy of your favour. May you receive them with kindness and be father, guide, and friend to them. From this moment I surrender to you my rights in them, but I ask you to practise forbearance toward any deficiencies which a father's indulgent eye may have overlooked, and in spite of these to continue your friendship toward one who values it so highly. I am with all my heart, dear friend, your most sincere friend

W. A. Mozart

Mozart's six great quartets dedicated to Haydn and published as his Op 10. The engraved title page of the original edition, 1785

Leopold also found that his son, along with all the most important people in Vienna, had become a Freemason. Freemasonry has never been so popular in Vienna before or since; but, for some reason, during the 1780s it flourished. What appealed to Mozart most about it was the importance Freemasons gave to friendship and to helping each other. Without the security of a court appointment, he needed something to fall back on. Nowadays, one cannot be both a Catholic and a Freemason, but in those days there was no rule against this, and Mozart was both.

Day after day Leopold saw his son repeat success after

Mozart's Masonic Funeral Music in C minor, K.477. Autograph facsimile, November 1785 (Tübingen, Universitätsbibliothek)

success. He loved hearing the applause, but the strain on an old man of such a hectic life was beginning to show. He wrote to Nannerl from Vienna (12 March 1785):

We never get to bed before one o'clock at night, never rise before nine, dine around two or half past two. The weather is filthy. There are concerts every day, lessons all the time, composing, and so on. Where can I go to be out of the way? If only the concerts were over. It is impossible to describe the fuss and the noise. In the time I have been here, your brother's pianoforte has been moved at least twelve times from the house to the theatre or to another house.

Leopold had to break off one letter suddenly 'because the masseur or the floor-waxer is dancing round the room and I cannot find a warm corner in the whole flat where I can write'. It must have been a noisy household anyway without any additions, for besides a little child, Mozart had a lively dog called Guckel, and a bird called Starl that he had purchased for a mere 34 Kreutzer. The bird learnt to whistle a theme from one of his piano concertos (the finale of the G major, K 453); this delighted Mozart.

Leopold, unable to stand the pace any longer, though still enjoying himself, left Vienna in May and returned to Salzburg and the hated Archbishop Colloredo. Though they did not know it when they all said good-bye, Mozart would never see his father, or Salzburg, again.

The Irish singer Michael Kelly has described what Mozart was like at that period. Kelly went to supper with the Mozarts, and noticed at once how passionately fond of Constanze Mozart was. After supper the young people started dancing, and Mozart joined them, leaving Constanze and Kelly talking to each other.

Madame Mozart told me, that great as his genius was, he loved dancing.

He was a remarkably small man, very thin and pale, with a profusion of fine fair hair, of which he was rather vain. He always received me with kindness and hospitality. He was remarkably fond of punch of which beverage I have seen him take copious draughts. He was also fond of billiards, and had an excellent billiard table in his house. Many and many a game have I played with him, but always come off second-best. He gave Sunday concerts, at which I was never missing. He was kind-hearted and always ready to oblige, but so very

Vienna, view of the Prater, one of the most popular spots in the capital and often viewed by the Emperor. Coloured engraving by Ludwig Janscha and Johann Ziegler, 1790

107

particular when he played, that if the slightest noise were made he instantly left off.

Mozart was very liberal in giving praise to those who deserved it; but he felt contempt for insolent mediocrity.

He liked people to be themselves, and not to pretend to be clever or more important than they actually were.

HERR UND MADAME LANGE
Mitglieder des K. K. National
Hoftheaters in Wien

Josef and Aloysia Lange. From an engraving by Daniel Berger after the drawing by Lange, 1785

Chapter 9

Figaro and *Don Giovanni*

'The best of all is when a good composer, who understands the stage and is talented enough to make sound suggestions, meets that true phoenix, an able poet'—Mozart to his father

During the spring and summer of 1785 Mozart was busy and Leopold had no letters from him at all. Finally he heard the reason: Mozart had started work on a new opera, *The Marriage of Figaro,* and was so excited by it that he had little time to do anything else.

The Marriage of Figaro was based on a play by a Frenchman called Beaumarchais which had been enormously popular in

The Marriage of Figaro Autograph facsimile of a page from Act III, sc. viii. The manuscript, originally in the Preussische Staatsbibliothek, Berlin, disappeared in 1945

Lorenzo da Ponte
(1749–1838)

Paris two years before. The story was about a poor writer called Figaro who in order to earn his living became a barber and valet to an aristocratic Spaniard. In the play, Figaro's most important speech is:

My lord Count, because you're a great aristocrat, you think yourself a great genius! . . . Nobility, fortune, rank, influence, all that makes one so proud! What did you do to earn so many advantages? You just gave yourself the trouble of being born and nothing more: for the rest, you're rather a commonplace person. Whereas I, lost in the common herd, have had to use more thinking and scheming to get on than has been spent governing the whole of Spain for the past hundred years!

This was a familiar feeling for Mozart too, and he was the ideal person to make the play into an opera. The libretto was by Lorenzo da Ponte, a flamboyant, energetic Italian poet who had been writing opera libretti in Vienna for some years, and to whom the Emperor had just given the post of official theatre poet. He was the best librettist in Vienna—witty, lively, a fine writer, and an excellent foil for Mozart. They worked well together, and formed a lasting and fruitful partnership: Mozart's three great Italian operas, *Figaro, Don Giovanni,* and *Così fan tutte,* all had libretti by da Ponte. It would be interesting to speculate on how different the whole history of opera might have been had it not been for this lucky meeting of minds.

Mozart worked at top speed on *Figaro,* composing at the same time other music for his concerts—concertos and arias, as well as an operetta in honour of an important court occasion.

At about the same time, early in 1786 (he was now thirty), Mozart acquired a brilliant new pupil: a boy of eight years old, called Johann Nepomuk Hummel, who, like the great composer himself, had started playing well upon the clavier at the age of four. Hummel's father described the encounter. Mozart's opening words, he recalled, were:

You know, my dear friend, I'm not very fond of teaching; it takes too much of my time and interrupts my composing. But let's see and hear what's in the boy and whether it's worth taking trouble with him—All right, sit down at the clavier and show us what you can do, he said to Nepomuk. The boy took out a few small pieces by Bach which he had practised well, and set them on the clavier. Mozart made no comment, and he began. Wolfgang had sat down beside me again, arms folded, and listened. He became more and more attentive, his expression keener; his eyes lit up with delight. During the playing he nudged me gently once or twice and nodded his head in approval. When my boy was finished with the Bach, Mozart put before him a none too easy composition of his own, to see how he did on sight-reading. It came off quite well. . . .

Mozart took the boy into his own home and treated him like a son. Johann learnt fast, and two years later was taken on a tour of Europe by his father, as Mozart himself had been taken when a boy. Johann Hummel became quite famous later on as a composer, pianist and teacher; and he owed everything to his kind and enthusiastic teacher.

Figaro was now finished, and after various delays was due to have its first performance on 28 April. Mozart was nervous, because his Italian enemies among the court musicians led by Salieri were determined to make the opera fail. They were all jealous of Mozart's increasing fame and reputation, and he knew they would stick at nothing. There were two other operas, one by Salieri, ready for presentation at the same time as Mozart's *Figaro,* and each composer claimed the right to be

Johann Nepomuk Hummel (1778–1837). An anonymous portrait in oils (Vienna, Gesellschaft der Musikfreunde)

first in the season. Mozart was so angry at all the intrigues that he swore he would put his opera on the fire if it was not done first. In the end the Emperor decided on *Figaro*, to the fury of the Italians, and the opera went straight into rehearsal at last.

Da Ponte's memories of the trouble that surrounded *Figaro* give a good idea of the kind of pettiness which Mozart had to endure:

Neither Mozart nor I was without well-founded fears that we might have to suffer fresh annoyances from these two good friends of ours [Salieri and Casti] . . . and a certain Bussani, who had a post as inspector of costumes and stage properties, and was jack of all trades save that of an honest man. Having heard that I had woven a ballet into my *Figaro*, he ran forthwith to the Count [Rosenberg] and in tone of amazed indignation cried:

'Excellency, the *signor poeta* has put a ballet in his opera!'

The Count sent for me at once and, frowning darkly, launched into this dialogue . . . :

'So, the *signor poeta* has used a ballet in *Figaro!*'

'Yes, Excellency.'

'The *signor poeta* does not know that the Emperor has forbidden dancing in his theatre?'

'No, Excellency.'

'In that case, *signor poeta*, I will tell you so now.'

'Yes Excellency.'

'And I will tell you further, *signor poeta*, that you must take it out! . . . Where is the scene with the dance?'

'Here it is, Excellency.'

'This is the way we do.'

Saying which, he took two sheets of my manuscript, laid them carefully on the fire, and returned the libretto to me:

'You see, *signor poeta*, that I can do anything!'

And he honored me with a second *Vade.*

I hurried to Mozart. On hearing my tale, he was desperate—he suggested going to the Count, giving Bussani a beating, appealing to Caesar, withdrawing the score. I had all I could do to calm him. But at length I begged him to allow me just two days' time, and to leave everything to me.

The dress rehearsal of the opera was to be held that day. I went in person to invite the Sovereign, and he promised to attend at the hour set. And in fact he came, and with him half the aristocracy of Vienna. The Abbé Casti likewise was in the royal party.

The first act went off amid general applause, but at the end of it there comes a pantomime scene between the Count and Susanna, during which the orchestra plays and the dance takes place. But the way His Excellency Can-All had adapted the scene, all one could see was the Count and Susanna gesticulating and, there being no music, it all looked like a puppet show. 'What's all this?' exclaimed the

Title page of the program of the premiere of *The Marriage of Figaro*

Manuscript from *The Marriage of Figaro*

The room in which Mozart wrote *The Marriage of Figaro*

Michael Kelly, Irish singer

Emperor to Casti, who was sitting behind him.

'You must ask the poet that!' replied the Abbé, with a significant smile.

His Majesty, therefore, sent for me; but instead of replying to the question put to me, I handed him my manuscript, in which I had restored the scene. The Sovereign glanced through it and asked why the dancers had not appeared. My silence gave him to understand that there was some intrigue behind it all. He turned to the Count [Rosenberg] and asked him to explain; and he, spluttering, said that the ballet had been left out because the opera had no dancers.

'But can't they be procured at some other theatre?' asked His Majesty.

Rosenberg answered that they could.

'Very well, let da Ponte have as many as he needs.'

In less than half an hour twenty-four dancers, what with extras, had come in. By the end of the second act, the scene that had been suppressed was in shape to be tried; and the Emperor cried:

'Oh, now it's all right!'

One of the singers was the Irishman Michael Kelly, who has left us long descriptions of the rehearsals and first performance of *Figaro:*

All the original performers had the advantage of the instruction of the composer, who transfused into their minds his inspired meaning. I never shall forget his little animated countenance, when lighted up with the glowing rays of genius—it is as impossible to describe it as it would be to paint sunbeams.

During all the rehearsals, Mozart was darting about in the wings, calling out 'Bravo! Bravo!' when someone sang an aria particularly well.

Then at last on 1 May at the Burgtheater came the *première,* and in spite of all the vicious plotting of the Italians, it was a magnificent success.

'At the end of the opera,' wrote Kelly, 'I thought the audience would never have done applauding and calling for Mozart; almost every piece was encored, which prolonged it nearly to the length of three operas (it already lasts at least 4 hours!) and induced the Emperor to issue an order on the second representation that no piece of music should be encored. Never was anything more complete than the triumph of Mozart.

Figaro was repeated nine times between May and December. Then another opera by someone else was performed, which was just as great a success, and Mozart's *Figaro* was forgotten by the fickle Viennese public for the next two years.

Top
Anna Selina (Nancy) Storace (1766–1817), the first Susanna in *Figaro.* She was a noted English soprano of Italian origin. Silhouette

Bottom
Michael Kelly as Busilio in *Figaro.* Silhouette

113

Vienna, the
Michaelplatz and the
Burgtheater where
Figaro was first
performed on 1 May
1786. The *Seraglio* was
also performed here in
1782, and *Così fan
tutte* was to be
premiered in 1790.
Coloured engraving,
anonymous

In fact, not Vienna but Prague, in Bohemia, was the first city
to recognise Mozart's true genius and treat him accordingly. In
Vienna there were other great composers, Gluck and Haydn
leading them, and Mozart was just regarded as one of many.
But in Prague he was regarded as the greatest of all, from the
moment the people of Prague heard the *Seraglio* in 1783 they
had ears for no other composer. When *Figaro* was first given in
Prague in December 1786 it created a greater sensation than
any opera ever had before. The theatre was packed out,
performance after performance; people even threw poems

Silhouettes of Haydn,
Gluck, Mozart and
Salieri, engraved by H.
Löschenkohl for the
*Osterreichischer
Nationalkalender*
of 1786

Haydn

Gluck

Mozart

Salieri

down from the gallery on to the stage in praise of the work and
the singers.

When Mozart heard of this triumph he decided to go to
Prague at once. 'Yesterday, January 11; our great and beloved
composer, Herr Mozart, arrived here from Vienna,'
announced a Prague newspaper. From then on Prague could
not see or hear enough of Mozart. Overwhelmed, he wrote to
Baron Gottfried von Jacquin, one of his pupils in Vienna:

Here they talk about nothing but *Figaro.* Nothing is played, sung or
whistled but *Figaro.* No opera is drawing like *Figaro.* Certainly a
great honour for me!

A public concert was arranged, and was packed to
overflowing. A contemporary reported:

By general request he . . . performed on the pianoforte at a grand
concert in the opera house. Never before had the theatre been so
crowded as it was on this occasion; never before had there been such
overwhelming and unanimous ecstasy as his divine playing aroused.

We truly did not know which we ought to admire the more, the extraordinary compositions or the extraordinary playing. Both together produced a total effect upon our souls which resembled a sweet enchantment. At the end of the concert, when Mozart improvised alone for more than half an hour, and our rapture reached its highest degree, the spell dissolved in a thunderous outpouring of applause. And in truth this improvisation surpassed all that anyone could imagine possible in the art of clavier playing, for the pinnacle of the art of composition was here united with sublime skill in performance. And certainly, just as this concert was unique to the people of Prague, Mozart must have counted this day among the finest in his life.

Another recalled:

Mozart. A so-called 'spurious' portrait by Anton Wilhelm Tischbein

116

View of Prague

The National Theater in Prague

SINFONIE

à grand orchestre

composée

par

W. A. Mozart.

× Œuvre 87.

Nº 1478. Prix f 3.

A Offenbach sur le Mein, chés J. André

Title page of the *Prague* symphony

Beethoven, about 1787

At the end of the concert Mozart improvised upon the fortepiano
for a good half-hour, thereby bringing the enthusiasm of the
delighted Bohemians to the highest pitch. As a result of the storm of
applause, he felt compelled to sit down at the clavier once more. The
torrent of this new improvisation had an even more powerful effect,
and the consequence was that he was overwhelmed for the third time
by the ardent audience. Once more Mozart reappeared. Sincere
gratification at the enthusiastic appreciation for his artistic
achievements radiated from his countenance. He began for the third
time with still higher inspiration, performed feats that had never been
performed before. Suddenly, out of the prevailing utter silence, a
loud voice in the *parterre* cried: 'From *Figaro!*' Whereupon Mozart
introduced the theme of that favorite aria '*Non più andrai
farfallone . . .*' and produced impromptu a dozen of the most
fascinating and artful variations, and thus, amid roars of jubilation,

117

concluded this remarkable exhibition of his art, which for him was certainly the most glorious in his life, and for the Bohemians, who were intoxicated with rapture, was surely the most enjoyable.

After a month of thunderous applause, and respect and affection shown to him everywhere, Mozart returned to Vienna with Constanze. Prague had given him a joyful new confidence, and something else: a commission to write a new opera, *Don Giovanni*, again with the libretto by Lorenzo da Ponte. Da Ponte, in his typically humorous way, later described how he wrote the libretto:

Don Giovanni, autograph facsimile of a page from Act II, No 25. (Paris, Bibliothèque du Conservatoire)

I sat down at my table and did not leave it for twelve hours continuous—a bottle of Tokay to my right, a box of Seville to my left, in the middle an inkwell. A beautiful girl of sixteen—I should have preferred to love her only as a daughter, but alas . . . !—was living in the house with her mother, my housekeeper, and would come to my

room at the sound of the bell. To tell the truth, the bell rang rather frequently, especially at moments when I felt my inspiration waning. She would bring me now a little cake, now a cup of coffee, now nothing but her pretty face, a face always gay, always smiling, just the thing to inspire poetical emotion and witty thoughts. I worked twelve hours a day every day, with a few interruptions, for two months on end; and through all that time she sat in an adjoining room, now with a book in hand, now with needle or embroidery, but ever ready to come to my aid at the first touch of the bell. Sometimes she would sit at my side without stirring, without opening her lips or batting an eyelash, gazing at me fixedly or blandly smiling, or now it would be a sigh or a threat of tears. In a word, this girl was my Calliope for those three operas, as she was afterwards for all the verse I wrote during the next six years. At first I tolerated such visits very often; later I had to make them less frequent in order not to lose too much time in amorous nonsense, of which she was perfect mistress. The first day, between the Tokay, the snuff, the coffee, the bell, and my young muse, I wrote the two first scenes of *Don Giovanni,* two more for the *Arbore di Diana,* and more than half of the first act of *Tarar,* a title I changed to *Assur.* I presented those scenes to the three composers the next morning. They could scarcely be made to believe that what they were reading with their own eyes was possible. In sixty-three days the first two operas were entirely finished and about two thirds of the last.

In that spring of 1787 a sixteen-year-old boy, short, stocky and dark, came to visit Mozart. He was Ludwig van Beethoven, and he had been sent to study under the great Mozart. But unfortunately after only two weeks he had to leave and go home because he had news that his mother was critically ill. Mozart realised how exceptionally talented young Beethoven was, but had little time to teach him, because he was working at top speed on *Don Giovanni.* The story that Mozart prophesied that Beethoven would 'make a noise in the world' is almost certainly apocryphal.

By now Mozart was working at a colossal pressure and his output was prodigious. Added to this were his domestic responsibilities—his wife, whose health was poor; the six babies who were born during the span of his married life; and the continual worry about money. The strain of it all made him ill again and for a time he had to stop working on *Don Giovanni.*

It was at this moment that he heard his father was seriously ill. The rift between them had widened over the years since Mozart's marriage and Leopold was leading a lonely life in Salzburg. They still exchanged letters, but not as frequently as before. On 4 April 1787, Mozart wrote his last letter to his father:

I hear that you are really ill. I need hardly tell you how greatly I am longing to receive some reassuring news from yourself. And I still expect it; although I have now made a habit of being prepared in all affairs of life for the worst. As death, when we come to consider it closely, is the true goal of our existence, I have formed during the last few years such close relations with this best and truest friend of mankind that his image is not only no longer terrifying to me, but is indeed very soothing and consoling! . . . I hope and trust that while I am writing this, you are feeling better. But if, contrary to all expectation, you are not recovering, I implore you . . . not to hide it from me, but to tell me the whole truth or get someone to write it to me, so that as quickly as is humanly possible I may come to your arms. I entreat you by all that is sacred—to both of us.

As a Catholic, living in an age when hygiene was unknown and death through disease an everyday occurrence, Mozart unquestioningly accepted it as a blessing ordained by God; one that must be borne with resignation and fortitude by the bereaved. In writing of death to his father in this way he showed a thoughtlessness which was entirely consistent with his deep religious beliefs, and with himself as an artist. A great artist is often insensitive to some aspects of human relationships. On 28 May Leopold died. Nannerl was with him at the end, so he was not alone, but Mozart was too ill to travel to Salzburg. He could not even attend the funeral.

In October Mozart returned to Prague to finish *Don Giovanni*, taking Constanze with him, but leaving his three-year-old son Karl behind in Vienna. The opera was due to be performed on 14 October, but it was not ready in time, and 29 October was fixed. Two days before the *première* Mozart still had not written the overture; his friends were frantic with worry. The more frantic they became, the more amused and calm was Mozart.

On the evening before the great day a good party was given during which Mozart enjoyed himself immensely and took no notice of various pointed remarks about finishing overtures.

Then at midnight he disappeared to write his overture; Constanze went with him, and so did a good big jug of punch. She kept him awake by telling him stories while he worked, but even so he dozed off for a couple of hours, he was so exhausted. At five in the morning Constanze woke him, and by seven o'clock the overture was written.

One thing to remember about the fantastic speed with which Mozart composed is this: *before* he wrote his music down it was always complete in his mind, so all he had to do was write down from memory what was already there.

The opera was received with wild enthusiasm; Prague again

went mad over Mozart's music. Mozart wrote:

October 29 my opera *Don Giovanni* had its first performance, and was received with the greatest applause. Yesterday it was given for the fourth time (this time for my benefit). I intend to leave here on the twelfth or thirteenth. . . . I wish my good friends . . . could be here for a single evening to share in my pleasure. Perhaps the opera will be given in Vienna after all. I hope so. Here they are doing their best to persuade me to stay another few months and write a couple more operas. Flattering as this offer is, however, I cannot accept it. . . . My great-grandfather used to say to his wife, my great-grandmother, and she to her daughter, my grandmother, and she in turn to her daughter, my mother, and she again to her daughter, my own sister, that it is a great art to speak well elegantly, but an art perhaps no less great to stop at the right time. So I intend to follow the advice of my sister as handed down from our mother, grandmother, and great-grandmother, and put an end not only to my moralistic digression, but to this whole letter.

On 15 November the famous opera composer, Gluck, had died. His position as court composer would have to be refilled, and Mozart rushed back to Vienna in the hope he would get the appointment. He knew that all the Italian musicians would be trying for it, too, and would do their utmost to prevent him getting it. He had to make the effort, however. This was perhaps at last his big chance of permanent employment at the Imperial Court.

Playbill for the first Viennese performance of *Don Giovanni*, 7 May 1788

This time his hopes were fulfilled. Wolfgang Amadeus Mozart was appointed the Imperial and Royal Court Composer at a small starting salary which just about paid the rent, but which at least was regular. At last, aged thirty-one, he had finally got the post Leopold had been so long hankering after for his son. It was sad that the old man had died six months too soon to see it happen.

The new court composer's opera *Don Giovanni* was performed the following spring in Vienna. At first the Viennese did not like the opera at all. The Emperor saw it and was asked what he thought. 'That opera is divine,' he said. 'I should even venture that it's more beautiful than *Figaro*. But such music is not meat for the teeth of my Viennese!' According to da Ponte, Mozart's reaction to this remark was to reply quietly: 'Give them time to devour it!'

Music-lovers in Vienna argued about *Don Giovanni*, and appealed to Haydn for his opinion. 'I cannot settle this quarrel,' he said in his kindly way. 'But I know this, that Mozart is the greatest composer now living in the world . . . For if every friend of music, particularly among the

Vienna, a view from the gardens of Neuwaldegg Castle. Coloured engraving by Ludwig Janscha, *c.* 1793

Decree appointing Mozart as Composer of the Imperial Chapel

Ballroom of the Imperial Palace in Vienna, where Mozart's dances were played

nobility, could grasp the incomparable works of Mozart with the depth of emotion and of musical understanding with which I grasp and feel them, nations would rival each other to have such a jewel within their walls.'

Lovers of Mozart's music insisted on *Don Giovanni* being repeated in Vienna for all its lack of success, and slowly but surely the Viennese came to like it more and more each time they heard it; in the end they decided it was one of the most beautiful operas that had ever been produced on any stage.

Chapter 10

Poverty and Death

'Mozart's influence transcends history'—Alfred Einstein

Mozart's new court appointment brought very little difference to his position: the money was not enough to live on, and the innumerable sets of dances and incidental pieces of music he was asked to write did nothing for his reputation. Once he sent the receipt for his salary back with a note saying: 'Too much for what I do—too little for what I could do.'

He and Constanze moved to a house slightly outside Vienna in June 1788, taking their son and their little daughter Theresa, who was now six months old. But ten days after they moved Theresa died. Though Mozart was both unhappy about this and worried because he was so short of money, in the next month or so he wrote his three last great symphonies, one after another. They were the E flat major (No. 39), the G minor (No. 40), and finally the C major (No. 41), which became known in the nineteenth century as the *Jupiter* symphony, each one conceived and written in the fullness of his mature inspiration, and all composed in under six weeks. This incredible feat of composition was perhaps his supreme achievement. One would never guess the troubles and miseries he was suffering while he composed these symphonies. His love of creating music could always make him forget the outside world.

The house in the country was not a success—Mozart felt he was too far out of the centre of Vienna, and he could not get pupils to come to him there. So they moved back into a flat in the city. (Mozart and Constanze had moved house eleven times since they married; no wonder their home life was so unsettled and chaotic.) Being back in the city made little difference to Mozart's income; he had a few pupils, but his concerts, which had always drawn full audiences in the past, were no longer popular. The fickle Viennese taste had changed. Mozart had to

The opening page of Mozart's last symphony, the *Jupiter*.

The manuscript, originally in the Preussische Staatsbibliothek, Berlin, disappeared in 1945. A reproduction, however, had already been published in 1923

125

A thematic list of
some of Mozart's most
popular works engraved
by Preston of London
in the 1790s or the
early 1800s (Ates
Orga)

borrow money from friends to keep going, and this depressed
him. He was reduced to writing letters like this one to the
friend who lent him money regularly during the last years of his
life, Michael Puchberg, a fellow Freemason:

Great God! I would not wish my worst enemy to be in my present
position. And if you, most beloved friend and brother, forsake me,
we are altogether lost, both my unfortunate and blameless self and
my sick wife and child. . . . I am coming to you not with thanks but
with fresh entreaties! Instead of paying my debts I am asking for
more money! . . . So it all depends, my only friend, upon whether
you will or can lend me another five hundred gulden. . . .

Prince Carl Lichnowsky
(1756–1814).
Oil-painting,
anonymous
(Czechoslovakia,
Schloss Hradeč)

He composed very little during that winter of 1788–9. He
was now thirty-three years old, and whereas most other
composers had financial security by the time they were that
age, Mozart was poorer than he had ever been. His golden
years in Vienna were over.

In the spring of 1789 a friend of Mozart's, Prince Carl
Lichnowsky, invited him to accompany him to Berlin, stopping
at Prague, Leipzig and Dresden on the way. Mozart leapt at
the chance of a concert-tour; he longed for a break from the
depression of Vienna.

128   Mozart, the last portrait.

St. Thomas Church and School in Leipzig

The Brandenburg Gate, Berlin

Mozart at the Berlin performance
of *The Abduction from the Seraglio*

The Bruhl Terrace in Dresden

He set out in April, in high spirits. He wrote Constanze long letters almost every day, telling her funny stories about what had been happening, and saying how much he was missing her. He and Prince Lichnowsky arrived in Leipzig at the end of April. Leipzig was Johann Sebastian Bach's city, and Mozart played Bach's own church organ, to his great delight. He was very excited at hearing some of Bach's music he had never heard before.

'Now here is something one can learn from!' he exclaimed and spent hours poring over sheets of Bach's music.

He gave a successful public concert in Leipzig, though he had trouble rehearsing the orchestra. He grumbled because everyone tried to play or sing things too quickly.

'They think that is going to make it fiery,' he said crossly. 'But if the fire isn't in the composition itself, racing through it will not put it in.'

Yet at the last rehearsal of his concert he surprised everyone by making the orchestra play it very fast. They soon lagged behind and got the tempo wrong.

'Again!' he shouted to the orchestra, stamping his foot. They began to get extremely angry with this pale-faced little man bullying them, and in rage played faster and more precisely. Mozart sighed with relief, and took the rest of the symphony at its normal speed. Afterwards, according to a contemporary witness, he explained to his friends: 'It wasn't just caprice on my part. I saw that most of the musicians were pretty old, and there would have been no end of dragging if I hadn't whipped them up at the start and made them angry. Then they did their best out of sheer pique!'

That particular concert was musically a great success; but financially, Mozart made nothing. On he went to Berlin, where an amusing thing happened. *Il Seraglio* was being performed at the national theatre; Mozart crept in at the back to listen. But he got so excited that without realising what he was doing, he edged his way to the front, humming the music to himself. He had no idea the whole audience was laughing at this odd little man. When the second violin played D sharp instead of D, Mozart could not restrain himself.

'Damn it all,' he shouted, '*will* you play D!'

Everyone looked up, startled, and then the word passed round like wildfire: 'Mozart is here!'

A month later he was back in Vienna; Mozart's only real success of the whole tour was a commission from the Berlin court to compose six string quartets and six piano sonatas. He set to work on these at once, but not for long; his next misfortune was that Constanze became seriously ill. He had to borrow a large sum of money again from the same faithful friend, Puchberg, to pay for the expensive cures the doctors had ordered for Constanze; his meagre court salary hardly covered basic living expenses. Constanze had gone to Baden for her health, and their son Karl had gone to boarding school, so Mozart was alone trying to work in Vienna during the summer. He did very little, but one good thing was offered him; he was asked to write another opera.

What was most worrying about Constanze was that she was pregnant during her illness. In November she had a baby girl, who died almost at once. Another blow; the Mozarts had now lost four babies altogether.

Mozart threw himself into composing his opera and tried to forget all his troubles; he had to borrow more money to tide him over until he was paid for the opera, to be called *Così fan tutte* (Italian for 'All Women Behave Thus'), again with a libretto by da Ponte. It was performed at the end of January 1790, and was an immediate success, after all the usual intrigues against it stirred up by Mozart's enemy Salieri; he spread slanderous stories about Mozart hoping that the Emperor would forbid its presentation.

Then in February the Emperor Joseph II died, and there were great changes in the court at Vienna. All court appointments naturally came to an end, and unless the new Emperor Leopold, Joseph's brother, re-established them, that was that. Mozart, like all the other court musicians, was hopeful for a post in the new régime.

Mozart went on hoping for a post all that year without any success, borrowing money from his staunch and long-suffering friend Puchberg in order to keep going. His only income came from his lessons, and all that money, and more, went on paying for Constanze's health cures in Baden.

Mozart himself was not well; he had bad headaches and colds, and could not sleep. Naturally enough, he composed very little that summer of 1790; it was the most miserable and depressing period of his life. This letter to Michael Puchberg shows the bad state he was in.

Vienna, 14 August 1790

Dear Friend and Brother,

Whereas I felt tolerably well yesterday, I am absolutely wretched today. I could not sleep all night for pain. Picture to yourself my condition—ill and consumed with worries and anxieties. Such a state quite definitely prevents me from recovering. In a week or a fortnight I shall be better off—certainly—but at present I am in want! Can you help me out with a trifle?

Manuscript from the opera *Cosi fan Tutte*

Romerberg Square in Frankfurt

The Holy Roman Emperor Leopold II

Engraving of the Emperor Leopold's coronation

The opening page of Mozart's String Quartet in D major, K.575, the first of the quartets written for the King of Prussia in June 1789: six were commissioned, only three were finished (London, British Museum)

But Mozart was an incurable optimist and when he decided to go to Frankfurt a month later he was sure his fortunes would change. He wrote to his wife in Baden: 'What a glorious life we shall have then! I will work—work so hard—that no unforeseen accidents shall ever reduce us to such desperate straits again. . . .'

He was going to Frankfurt for the coronation of Leopold II as Holy Roman Emperor: fifteen musicians of the Vienna court orchestra led by Salieri had been chosen to go, but Mozart was not among them. Undaunted, he decided to go at his own expense. To buy a carriage, he had to pawn his silver. He also had to borrow money from Puchberg.

The programme of
Mozart's concert at
the Schauspielhaus,
Frankfurt, 15 October
1790

Mit gnädigster Erlaubniß
Wird Heute Freytags den 15ten October 1790.
im grosen Stadt-Schauspielhause
Herr Kapellmeister Mozart
ein grosses

musikalisches Konzert

zu seinem Vortheil geben.

Erster Theil.

Eine neue grose Simphonie von Herrn Mozart.

Eine Arie, gesungen von Madame Schick.

Ein Concert auf dem Forte-piano, gespielt von Herrn Kapellmeister
Mozart von seiner eigenen Komposition.

Eine Arie, gesungen von Herrn Cecarelli.

Zwenter Theil.

Ein Concert von Herrn Kapellmeister Mozart von seiner eigenen Komposition.

Ein Duett, gesungen von Madame Schick und Herrn Cecarelli.

Eine Phantasie aus dem Stegreife von Herrn Mozart.

Eine Symphonie.

Die Person zahlt in den Logen und Parquet a fl. 45 kr.
Auf der Gallerie 24 kr.

Billets sind bey Herrn Mozart, wohnhaft in der Kahlbechergasse Nro. 167. vom Donnerstag Nachmittags und Freytags Frühe bey Herrn Cassirer Scheidweiler und an der
Casse zu haben.

Der Anfang ist um Eilf Uhr Vormittags.

M.150.

He gave a concert in Frankfurt, which as usual brought
plenty of praise but no money. Seeing that there was no hope
of further success in Frankfurt, he went on to Mannheim,
where he knew *Figaro* was being performed. Mannheim had
changed a lot in ten years, and no one recognised Mozart. He
went up to the theatre door and asked an actor if he could
listen to the rehearsal of *Figaro*. The actor thought he was a
tailor's apprentice and tried to send him packing.

132

Emanuel Schikaneder (1751–1812), German actor, playwright and theatrical manager. Apart from providing the libretto for *The Magic Flute*, he also worked with Beethoven

'Why, surely you will permit Mozart to listen?' said Mozart. The actor was extremely embarrassed and took him at once to meet the orchestra and cast.

Back in Vienna, Mozart found two invitations to go to London. He had always wanted to return there and decided he would go when he had finished the new opera he was working on. He was sure he would find real honour and glory in England.

One of the invitations was from the London Opera:

Through a person attached to His Royal Highness, the Prince of Wales, I have learned of your intention to visit England. Because I am appointed to meet men of talent personally, and at present am in a position to be of advantage to them, I offer you, sir, the place of composer in England. If therefore you are able to come here at the end of this coming December 1790, and remain until the end of June 1791, and during this time to compose at least two serious or comic operas, as the management should decide, I am prepared to offer you three hundred pounds sterling. You will also be free to write compositions for any other concert hall, other theatres being excepted. If this contract appeals to you and you are in a position to accept it, please do me the honour of replying by return post, and this letter will then serve as a contract.

Before he could accept, however, he had to finish his new opera, *The Magic Flute.* The idea of writing his opera came from a friend of Mozart's called Schikaneder; the libretto, in German, was by Schikaneder himself, and told the fairy-story of how a magic flute in the hands of the hero, Tamino, took him safely through dangers to enlightment, securing the love of Pamina on the way. Mozart was nervous about the whole opera.

Early 19th century set for *La Clemenza di Tito*, originally produced in Prague, 6 September 1791, to mark the coronation of Leopold II as King of Bohemia

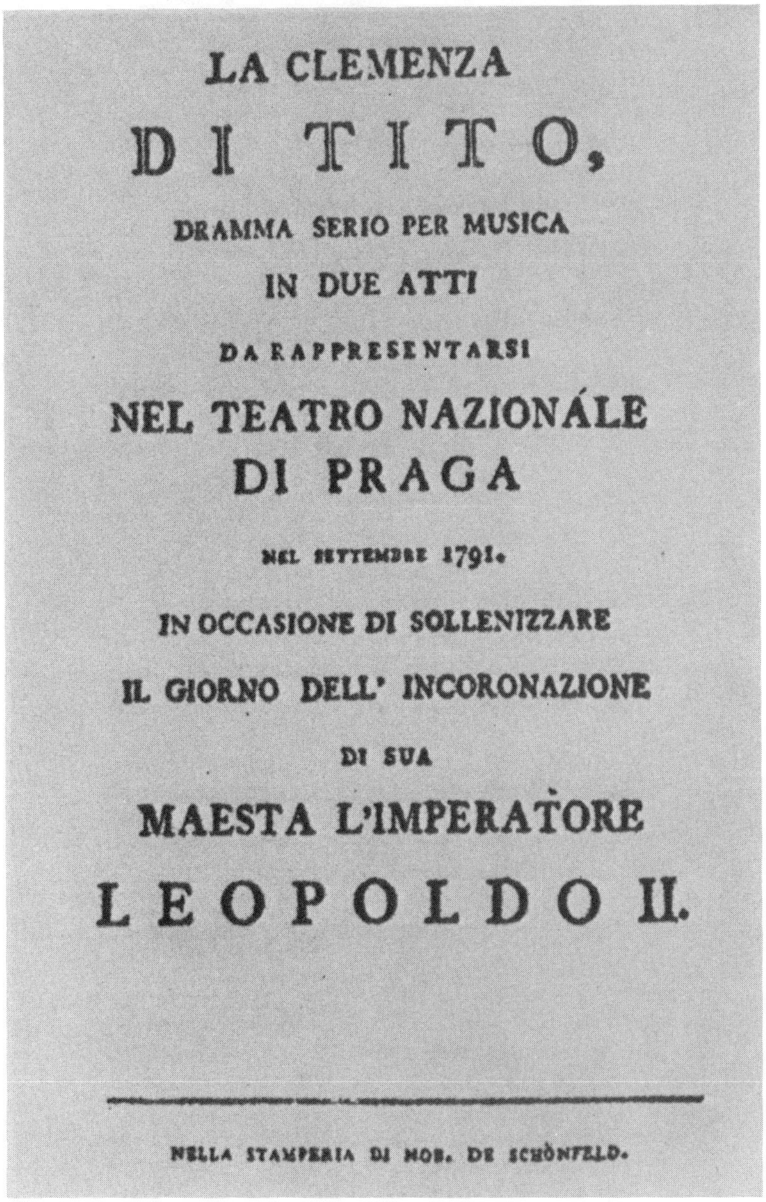

LA CLEMENZA
DI TITO,
DRAMMA SERIO PER MUSICA
IN DUE ATTI
DA RAPPRESENTARSI
NEL TEATRO NAZIONÁLE
DI PRAGA
NEL SETTEMBRE 1791.
IN OCCASIONE DI SOLLENIZZARE
IL GIORNO DELL' INCORONAZIONE
DI SUA
MAESTA L'IMPERATORE
LEOPOLDO II.

NELLA STAMPERIA DI MOR. DE SCHÖNFELD.

Title page of the libretto
at the premiere of *La Clemenza di Tito*

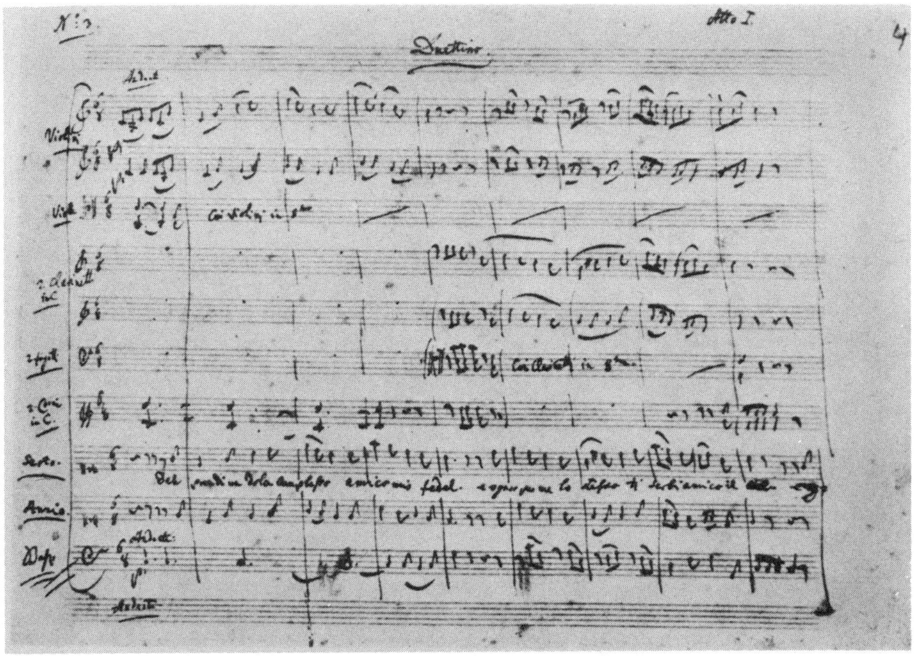

Manuscript from the opera

Program for the Vienna premiere of *The Magic Flute*

Title page of the libretto

Schikaneder in the rôle of Papageno at the first performance of *The Magic Flute.* Engraving, 1791

'If we have a flop, I can't do anything about it, for I've never composed a magic opera.' So that he would not be distracted, he composed in a little wooden summer house specially put up for him near the theatre. Constanze was away in Baden, and he was always depressed without her. She was expecting another baby, and what with this and the usual worries about lack of money, it is a wonder Mozart could compose at all.

In July 1791, Constanze gave birth to a little son, and this time the baby lived. Now Mozart had two children, Karl and Franz Xavier Wolfgang. At about the same time as Franz's birth a very odd thing happened.

A tall gaunt stranger, wearing grey, called one day on Mozart, and left an anonymous letter asking him to write a Requiem. Mozart, ill and depressed, was deeply worried by this unknown man, who kept calling on him and demanding the Requiem.

He wrote to da Ponte in September:

My head is confused. I can think only with difficulty, and cannot free my mind of the image of the Unknown. I constantly see him before me; he pleads with me, presses me, and impatiently demands the work from me. I am continuing with it because the composing is less tiring than doing nothing. Besides, I have nothing more to fear. I can feel from my present state that the hour is striking. I am on the point of expiring. My end has come before I was able to profit by my talent. And yet life has been so beautiful; my career began under such fortunate auspices. But no one can change his fate. No one can count his days; one must resign oneself. What Providence determines will be done. I close now. Before me lies my swan song. I must not leave it incomplete.

He felt his end was near, and that he was composing his own Requiem. He was not to know that the strange man in grey had come from a nobleman who wanted to pass off Mozart's composition as his own.

The *première* of *The Magic Flute* was set for 30 September; Mozart wrote the last notes for the opera on 29 September. He was sick, and lived on medicine; he had had so many failures and disappointments recently that he had lost his gay confidence. But he need not have worried; *The Magic Flute* was a huge success, and day after day the applause increased.

Mozart's heart lightened; suddenly the future seemed more hopeful again. Even composing the Requiem did not depress him for a while; and he planned to go to England the following year, 1792. Life was good again, even though Constanze, who came to Vienna for the *première* of *The Magic Flute,* had gone

135

The final two pages of Mozart's thematic *Catalogue of all my works*, begun in 1784. The last entries are for *The Magic Flute*, *La Clemenza di Tito*, the Clarinet Concerto in A major and the Masonic Cantata, K.623. (Vienna, Österreiche Nationalbibliothek)

back to Baden with the baby. Mozart wrote her long happy letters, full of jokes and his usual nonsense. Even Salieri, his old enemy, had now become his friend and was enthusiastic about the new opera, shouting 'Bravo' from the audience at all the parts he particularly liked.

When Constanze returned to Vienna in early November she realised that Mozart was a very sick man indeed. He was weak, and suffered from fainting fits; this made him sure he was being poisoned. All the old fears that the Requiem was to be his own requiem were back; he was certain death was near.

Constanze tried to stop him working too hard and did her best to cheer him up. For a day or two he was his old self, and laughed at his fear of poisoning. But on 20 November he collapsed again, and had to go back to bed. His hands and feet became swollen, and he could no longer move them. He was continually sick.

All the Weber family came to see him, to his great delight. However weak he was, he loved seeing his friends, and they stayed by him. On 4 December he even took up the music of the Requiem again, and sang parts of it with his friends. He

Frontispiece of the first score of the Requiem

Manuscript of the "Lachrymosa" from the Requiem, the last music Mozart wrote

Mozart. The frontispiece
to an obituary notice,
1793. Engraving by
Clemens Kohl

gave one of them, his pupil Süssmayr, strict instructions about
how to finish the Requiem, as he was sure now he would never
be able to do it himself.

He grew weaker and weaker all that day, and died at
fifty-five minutes past midnight: it was 5 December 1791. His
last act was to try and make the sound of the drums in his
Requiem. His last breath was his music: then Wolfgang
Amadeus Mozart was dead.

Constanze Mozart.
Portrait by Hans
Hansen, 1802

Karl Thomas Mozart

Wolfgang Amadeus Xavier Mozart

The house were Mozart died

Epilogue

Mozart's funeral was both simple and cheap. Constanze was poor, and also it was the custom to have no elaborate ceremonies at that time in Vienna. Many people had come and wept outside the house when they heard that Mozart was dead; but at the actual funeral there was only a small handful of family and friends, among them Salieri. Constanze was not there (women did not attend funeral processions) and indeed was not to visit the site until as late as 1808. But she mourned her husband's death deeply and sincerely; aged only twenty-eight, she had lost her 'beloved husband Mozart, who cannot be forgotten by me and all of Europe'.

On that winter day no one followed the coffin to the grave. Mozart was buried in a common pauper's grave without a witness, and no cross was put on the place. No one ever knew where his body lay; he was neglected during his life, and neglected at his end. But his music is with us for as long as we have ears to listen.

'Posterity will not see such a talent as his for the next hundred years'—Haydn

Volti Subito

Nachricht.

Donnerstag den 10ten März 1785. wird Hr. Kapellmeister Mozart die Ehre haben in dem

k. k. National-Hof-Theater

eine

grosse musikalische Akademie

zu seinem Vortheile

zu geben, wobey er nicht nur ein neues erst verfertigtes Forte piano - Konzert spielen, sondern auch ein besonders grosses Forte piano Pedal beym Phantasieren gebrauchen wird. Die übrigen Stücke wird der grosse Anschlagzettel am Tage selbst zeigen.

141

Index
Illustrations are indicated by **bold** *type*

142

143

Monument to Mozart in the cemetery where he was buried

ILLUSTRATIONS ADDED FOR THE EXPANDED EDITION

In creating this expanded edition, more than seventy-five illustrations have been added as unnumbered pages at various places within the text. Following is a key to those insertions.